Christ 2.0

Was Jesus an Egyptian Pharaoh?

Horus Michael

Christ 2.0

Was Jesus an Egyptian Pharaoh?

Horus Michael

The Testament of
Horus Christ

Book 1: Asaris

Chapter 1:

1

3400 years ago, in the House of Amenophis, called Amonhotep Nebmaatra, dwelled a servant called Yu-seph. His foreign name was **Jo-Seph**, and his Egyptian name was originally Yu-yaph, or Yu-ya. He was a **descendant of Abraham of Babylon** (Aram).

2

Yu-seph was the **father of Tiye**, a commoner, who became the wife of Amenophis. Amenophis was the father of Thutmosis (Thutmose), Smenkhkara, and Amenophis 4. One of whom had a son named **Tutankhaton**. Amenophis was a **descendant of** Thutmose Menkheperra, (**King David** of the **tribe of Judah of Canaan**, according to the **Book of Osman**).

3

Tutankhaton was **an incarnation of Horus**, the heir of Asaris, who was the First King of Upper Egypt, then known as **Kemt**. Asaris was the First to be called **KRST**, or **Christ**, a word that means "burial" in a tomb.

4

Asaris (Osiris) was the **King of Kings,** the Lord of Lords of Kemt. He **civilized or conquered the World** with his knowledge; this followed the period known as the **Ice Age.** He introduced Agriculture (Farming) to the World, wrote Laws, he organized religion, taught Geometry, Music and the Arts.

5

Asaris sadly was murdered by his envious brother **Set** upon returning home. Set had asked Asaris to participate in a Magic Trick on his performance stage. Asaris entered a chest that was designed to Asaris' exact measurements. The chest was nailed shut and dropped into the Nile River, where it flowed downstream North to the Mediterranean Sea, until it washed up on the shores of Byblos in Phoenicia.

6

The chest became part of a tree at Byblos, probably a Cedar tree or Tamarisk. A King of Byblos cut the tree down to make a pillar for his Palace. The wife of Asaris, Aset (Isis) searched for the chest. She ordered the pillar to be opened upon finding it. The corpse of Asaris was then revealed.

7

Aset fanned air into Asaris' lungs by using her **angelic wings** until he resurrected. Upon his resurrection, Asaris and Aset mated. Nephthys also mated with Asaris.

8

Months later, Asaris and his family returned to Egypt. Asaris' first born son was **Horus** (from Aset); **Anubis** was his second born son (from Nephthys).

9

Set had usurped the throne of Asaris and ruled Egypt with an iron fist. He undid peace treaties, inspired Cannibalism and meat-eating (*Asaris was a vegetarian*), and conquered with Earthquakes and Storms. Set was the God of the Desert, Storms and Chaos.

10

Young Horus challenged Set's domain. When Set saw Asaris still lived, he grabbed a lance and killed him, this time he dismembered Asaris' body and scattered the parts all over the land. This made it difficult for Asaris to resurrect again. Set then pursued the young Horus, who fled into the Delta with his mother Aset.

11

Years later when Set returned to the Upper Kingdom of Egypt, Horus was old enough to challenge Set's rule. During his childhood Aset educated the young Horus. Thoth was his teacher, and his younger brother Anubis was his Physician.

12

There are many recorded phases or forms of Horus known in Egypt. Each was venerated as a separate Horus, representing one aspect of his nature or epoch in life.

13

Horus and Set battled for control of Egypt. Sometimes this was in a marshland where Set became a Hippopotamus or crocodile and attacked Horus while in a Papyrus boat. These battles are known as the Battles of Light vs. Darkness (Good vs. Evil). In later cultures they are the battles of Archangel Michael vs. Satan the Dragon, or Hercules vs. the Dragon. Sometimes each won, other times each lost a battle, but the war was ongoing.

14

In one battle Horus lost an eye. In another it was both eyes. His eyes were repaired by Thoth and returned to Horus. His eye was the *Eye of Sacrifice* (Wadjet Eye), as compared to the *Body of Christ*.

15

The last battle was in the Court of Asaris, where each participant represented why either was worthy enough to be King of Egypt. Asaris' body was searched for by Aset and reassembled by Horus, then he resurrected upon receiving an *Emerald Heart Scarab* amulet. Asaris was the Judge of the actions of the Living, and became King of Heaven.

16

Horus was decreed the winner of the Court process, and became King of Upper & Lower Egypt. Set lost and was beheaded. Set became the Defender of Ra's Celestial Boat in the Afterlife, where it was under constant attack by the Immortal Worm, Apophis, when Ra traveled there at night. Asaris' tomb was the Pyramid above the *Valley of the Kings* in Upper Egypt.

17

The *Eye of Sacrifice*, the Wadjet Eye, was a divine offering to Lord Asaris and could be used to symbolize any offering to the dead, such as Food & Drink (Bread and Wine), cloth or clothing, incense, and technology. This was kept on an altar to Asaris with one of his representations (statues) on the altar.

18

Horus became King of the Two Lands, and he ruled with wisdom and justice. He mated Hathor (*Goddess of Love*) and had 4 sons – **Duamutef, Qebehsenwf, Amseti, and Hapy** – who protected bodily organs in the Canopic Chest in the tomb of Asaris, or those of his followers. The chest that Asaris was entrapped in became known as a Coffin or Mummy Case. Erecting a tree on his birthday represented the Tree of Asaris, which became the Djed Pillar of Asaris. Offerings were placed at the base of the tree/pillar.

19

Asaris first resurrected in the Spring time (Season of Planting), near the Spring Equinox. His second resurrection was in June, or the Summer Solstice. This was moved to the Winter Solstice by later cultures.

The Egyptian Calendar had 360 days of 10 day weeks each. 5 days are added to this in the form of 5 birthdays of the family of Asaris. The birthdays are remembered in later cultures after the Winter Solstice, on December 25. Following this by one week is New Year's Day. On the birthdays of his family are given offerings to the participants of the celebration.

Once Evil has been vanquished Asaris returns to Earth to reestablish his Kingdom. This idea became the *Return of Christ* prophecy.

Reference: (John 14:6); (John 11:25)

"I am the way, the truth and the life..." &

*"I am the **resurrection** and the **life**, he that **believes in me**, though was dead, yet shall live..."*

Osiris (Asaris) was the **god of resurrection** and **Life**, and said *"Whoever believes in me shall live forever."*

https://en.wikipedia.org/wiki/Osiris

http://www.msn.com/en-us/news/world/5000-year-old-nativity-scene-reportedly-found-in-egypt/ar-BBxv6b3?li=BBnb7Kz

Chapter 2:

1

Tutankhaton ruled Egypt with wisdom and Divine Will also called *Egyptian Magic.* He could be angry at times, so his counselor was General Horemhab, who was his designated heir. Tutankhaton was married to his sister Ankhesenpaaton, in the fashion of Asaris and Aset, whom were also siblings.

2

Tutankhaton inherited an Egypt that was in a state of Civil War. His ancestor Amenophis 4 changed his name to Akhenaton, and taught that the Sun was God. Akhenaton built open-ceiling Temples so he could watch the Sun "drink its liquid offerings" daily as proof the Sun was God – as no statues could do that. The Egyptians made offerings to statues because they *summoned the souls* of the Gods *into* the statues. No one actually worshiped statues or idols, or so it appeared by outsiders.

3

Tutankhaton's mother was Meritaton. She was a *young* Queen during a time of civil strife, under Akhenaton.

4

Queen Meritaton's husband was Smenkhkara, one of the Kings who ruled during or just after the death or exile of Akhenaton. His full name was Smenkhkara Djoser-kheperu; abbreviated it is Djos(er)-Khep(eru), or Djos-Khep (**Joseph**). Meritaton abbreviated is Mery(t-aton); (**Mary**).

5

Queen Meritaton was impregnated by the soul of AmonRa in her Palace. AmonRa is the **God** of the Egyptians, the ancestor of Asaris. Those who are impregnated by the soul of God are called Virgins, as the father was not mortal or known. *Virgin also means youthful.*

6

When Tutankhaton was educated about the State of Affairs, **at age 12, he entered the Temples** of AmonRa at Karnak, Upper Egypt. He learned all he needed. So he changed the situation with wisdom and urgency. He changed the religion from Sun Worship to Traditional religion, and his names from Tutankhaton to Tutankhamon. He moved the Capital back to Thebes in the South and Mennofer (Memphis) to the North.

Ref: (Luke 2:41-52)

7

Tutankhamon found the old Temples in ruins, overcome with weeds and decay. He rebuilt the damaged Temples and built new ones. He wrote new laws and hired new priests. He built golden statues, ships for trading, and vineyards. To do this he needed revenue, so he attacked the weakened Border States with his Armies (*and Egyptian Magic*), and exacted **Tribute** (*spoils of war, or tax*) from them.

8

Tutankhamon imprisoned the people responsible for the destruction of the Temples, the followers of Aton. These people became the Habiru (Hebrews), a word meaning "outcast, wanderer or criminal." **The brother of Akhenaton whom was exiled was Thutmosis.** This brother would have been King in place of Akhenaton, had he not killed an Egyptian and was exiled *before* Akhenaton came to power. Because Akhenaton was against the Gods of Egypt, and AmonRa, the names of other Gods was stripped from names of the people, so Thutmosis became known simply as Mosis (**Moses**). So Moses became aware of the situation with the Habiru in Egypt.

9

    Towards the end of Tutankhamon's reign, his wife became notified of a mistress who was vying for attention. His wife, Ankhesenamon, wrote to the Hittites (a northern Superpower), saying her husband died and she wanted a replacement. When Tutankhamon discovered the letters, he ordered Horemhab to intercept the Hittite Prince that was to wed the Queen and become King of Egypt.

10

    While Horemhab was away, Tutankhamon was assassinated by usurpers to the throne, allied to Ankhesenamon. The soul of AmonRa was not pleased, so he resurrected Tutankhamon. Vizier Ay was the leader of this rebellion, whom Ankhesenamon had the letters sent by. So after Tutankhamon returned to life, he had Ay executed and his body stored in a tomb with a false wall built there to conceal it. Tutankhamon then ruled as King Ay and was still married to Ankhesenamon. The tomb mural in his tomb shows this.

11

So Tutankhamon as King Ay ruled for four more years until Horemhab returned to Egypt, while overseeing the affairs of State. King Ay died in a hunting accident four years after his resurrection, and his tomb was moved to the one containing the wall mural with Ay as his heir.

12

Horemhab returned to Egypt and was told that "Vizier Ay killed Tutankhamon" so Horemhab persecuted the remains of "King Ay" all over Egypt. He destroyed all trace of King Ay, his sarcophagus and tomb, temples, and statuary. On official records he claimed direct ancestry from Amenophis (Amonhotep Nebmaatra), ignoring all the others. His heir was Ramses the first.

13

Thutmosis, as Moses, returned during the later part of Pharaoh Horemhab's reign. Moses demanded the prisoners of Aton be released. Horemhab did not recognize this person, so he refused. Moses used Egyptian Magic to intimidate the Pharaoh. Akhenaton was the first King to call himself "Pharaoh."

14

The intimidations from Moses were acts of Nature known to Egyptians. Moses made the waters of the Nile undrinkable for several weeks. He caused man and beast to have cysts and lice. He caused frogs and locusts to fester in the fields. Darkness blotted out the Sun. Volcanic ash rained down from the sky as hot hail. Etc.

15

Pharaoh Horemhab did not budge. So he ordered the firstborn of the Atonists be killed. Moses responded by **cursing the heir of Pharaoh** with his Egyptian Magic. This curse killed Horemhab's unborn child, as known by his tomb wherein his pregnant wife was buried. **It also cursed** Pharaoh Tutankhamon whom was already dead by this time. Thus is why Tutankhamon is a cursed Pharaoh.

16

Horemhab released the prisoners, and later changed his mind and pursued them. Moses used the spell for moving waters as known in the Old Kingdom or Pyramid Age. This spell opened a path in the Sea of Reeds for an escape route, before closing on the incoming Egyptian chariots.

The Atonists under Moses wandered the region in Sinai for 4 years, not 40. There is a **ten-fold error in their Book**, such that the years of imprisonment were 43 years not 430 years. The Atonists formed a new country called Israel and Judea. The son of Ramses the first was called Sety. His grandson was Ramses 2 the Great, whose son **Merenptah conquered Israel,** as known on his Stele tablet. The Israelites never mentioned this in their Book. Of course their Book also mentioned the Egyptians had "**wagons and silver money**" during the time of Joseph; Egyptians did **not have wagons** only chariots, and **silver money** was invented 1000 years later.

The title NFR-NTR or **Good God** is used by Tutankhamon as a **title**. Normally if a ruler is uncertain about their legitimacy this title is presented, as with the heirs of Akhenaton. Christians said "God is Good." Ramses the Great had a title applied to him, "AA NTR" or "the Great God." In Islam, "God is Great!" **Both titles are Egyptian in origin**.

Chapter 3:

1

On December 25 during the reign of Caesar, the soul of AmonRa impregnated a virgin woman named Mary and she gave birth to Christ. Though, the woman may have been a Priestess of Vesta, or a *Vestal Virgin*, a sacred woman in Rome. Vestals could not be pregnant as this violated the Roman Laws, because Vestals were required to be *Chaste and Pure*.

2

Wise men from the East saw the Star of Christ's birth and went looking for it, said to number 3. If so, the 3 Wise Men – called the Three Kings – were actually the 3 Kings of the Pyramids of Giza, Egypt because the 3 Pyramids are in the night sky as *Orion's Belt*. The star appeared in the Constellation **Virgo**, *the Virgin*, appearing over a *Manger*. On Earth this meant within a **Mastaba**, or trapezoid shaped tomb in Egypt following the line from the 3 Pyramids. This line led to Saqqara to the Mastaba of Shepseskaf, of the 4th Dynasty. A **Mastaba** resembles a Manger.

3

The new born Christ was named *after* (Djed-ka-Ra) **Isesi**, a King whose Pyramid was nearby the Mastaba in Saqqara. His original name was revealed in a vision as being *Immanuel*. In Roman (Latin) the name was spelled **Iesus**. In Greek it is JESUS. The Greek word for "burial in a tomb" was Christ, from the Egyptian word QRST or KRST, as a Mastaba is a tomb. So the child was later to be known as JESUS the Christ. He was called this *before* he died.

4

Inside the Mastaba tomb were **burial offerings** for the dead Pharaoh Shepseskaf, in the form of **Gold, Frankincense and Myrrh**. The Pharaoh Isesi of the 5th Dynasty once raided the nations of Punt for **Myrrh** and Nubia for **gold**. He also raided Canaan.

5

Jesus was born in **Bethlehem**, which meant "**House of Bread**" in Hebrew & Aramaic. The House of Bread **in Egypt** was the **word for** *Offerings Chamber* in the tomb. It is also a city in Judea.

6

Jesus the Christ lived in Egypt for a short time as recorded in his Book. What he did there was not recorded. The story of Horus when compared to that of Jesus seems *plagiarized* but Horus existed thousands of years *before* Jesus lived. The Egyptians accepted the new religion because it was an **updated form** of their beliefs.

7

Jesus acquired **authority** following his purification rite or Baptism whereby a white soul (Ba) was seen entering him, so someone believed this was special. A Divine soul (NTR) is not white, but of *Emerald Fire*. The *Burning Bush* which Moses met was of this nature. Divine souls are visible to their incarnated forms when in total darkness or resting.

8

Once he **acquired authority over the spirits of Earth and Life**, he could heal people by casting out "unclean spirits." He also could raise the dead by calling forth the souls of the dead and returning them to Earth. This authority is spiritual in nature. He was the *Son of God*, just as the Pharaohs are *Sons of AmonRa*, as a **religious title**.

9

Because Jesus became overly popular the Roman Government sought to arrest him after the Jewish authorities believed he was transgressing their laws. Jesus would perform miracles as a distraction. Eventually they caught up to him and arrested Jesus. The Romans were asked to intervene, but decided to crucify him anyway.

10

Jesus was taken prisoner, mocked and tortured with a flail or scourge, and crucified on a wooden plank aside 2 thieves facing the evening Sun. After **he drank a sedative**, his soul briefly left him, and he **appeared dead**. His body was taken down and placed in a tomb. His soul later returned and he awoke, **as if** resurrected.

11

He moved the stone away from his tomb and closed it, and then he went to visit his followers to say he resurrected. He showed them his wounds and his wholeness. The sedative he took was powerful enough to stop his heartbeat or slow it into hibernation. It was mixed with old wine, or vinegar, with hyssop.

Jesus lingered for 40 days and ascended to Heaven, according to his Book. 40 days is the time it took for mummification, followed by a Night Boat ritual whereby the soul ascended to Heaven. Jesus *could have* moved away from the region, took a boat from Rome and traveled to Central America to educate the people in the form of **Quetzalcoatl**, whom was a *"bearded man from the East"* who educated the Toltec Civilization (**as Asaris**).

[Mark 16:36 (Vinegar) 16:37 (Jesus cried out and gave up the ghost); Luke 23:36; St John 19:29-30.]

https://en.wikipedia.org/wiki/Djedkare_Isesi

https://en.wikipedia.org/wiki/Pyramid_of_Djedkare-Isesi

Reference: (Matthew 4:1-11)

When Jesus was in the wilderness (Desert) for 40 days/nights, this could be during a funeral for someone in Egypt. The word "Satan" (who tempted Jesus in the Wilderness) is an anagram of "Sata" from Chapter 87 of the Egyptian funeral text. Sata is a serpent with legs, same as Satan (*Genesis*).

Chapter 4:

1

Some 2000 years *after* the resurrection of Christ the tomb of Tutankhamon was *opened* in Egypt. The soul of Tutankhamon was *awakened* when his name was first called in 1917; he fell asleep once his *recent incarnation* (**Napoleon I**) died in the 1800s Common Era. He had opened the tombs of the Ancient Egyptians and began Egyptology, waiting for his personal tomb to be opened like a *Time Capsule*.

2

In 1922 the tomb was opened and his soul was freed. The people who opened it did not all have reservations about the discovery. Some wanted to profit from it, or keep parts of it as *compensation* for the excavation. One such person was the Earl of Carnarvon, an Englishman (***Napoleon had issues with England***).

3

The soul of Tutankhamon was insulted by comments made in the public. "Tut, tut!" was one such insult. This happened in the Media and in private.

4

It wasn't long before Tutankhamon' s soul had his revenge against the rudeness and carelessness of the living. Moderns forgot the ways of the Ancients, so they dismiss supernatural events as being common or unimportant misfortune.

5

Lord Carnarvon cut himself while shaving and acquired blood poisoning. A water-boy in the tomb was bitten by a cobra, and the Archaeologist Howard Carter had a canary in the tomb, killed by a cobra. Canaries in the tomb were there to detect poison gas. Cobras existed in Egypt as common in tombs. Numerous others related to the discovery died mysteriously after Carnarvon died on April 5, 1923. All of Cairo's electricity went dark, and his dog in England howled at the Moon and died at the same moment. Howard Carter was spared because he had honest intentions. The media believed this was an *Ancient Curse.*

6

Tutankhamon was done safeguarding his tomb, so he looked around for something to do since he was awake. He decided to be alive again, and found a suitable family.

7

His recent life was a **French Emperor** and Conqueror. Tutankhamon dreamed a separate incarnation (life appears like a dream sometimes), as *President Abraham Lincoln*. His new life was John Fitzgerald Kennedy, or "Jack."

8

Jack was a **blue-eyed incarnation of Asaris**. Jack served in the American Navy as a boat captain, whose boat was wrecked during the War. He saved his crew by swimming to an island, and earned a medal for this. He later became interested in Politics and the Media.

9

Jack became a USA Senator before becoming its President. His "**Harem**" of Hollywood females affected his duties as President. The President lives in a building called The White House (*Pharaoh or Palace*). His White House was decorated in **French Empire** furnishings by his wife, Jacqueline, a French woman who resembled Ankhesenamon. He also felt like a "King Arthur" while in office.

10

Jack helped with Civil Rights legislation, created the Peace Corps, and desired Space Exploration and Psychic Warfare. He had a problem with Russia that started the main element of the Cold War era (**Napoleon had issues with Russia**). Like Asaris, Jack was murdered and so was forced to reincarnate as an Avenger Form of Horus. The fact his other family members had misfortune whenever seeking glory is the *Kennedy Family Curse*, an offshoot of the *Curse of Tutankhamon*.

11

Jack wanted to be a Writer, not President. His sister Kathleen convinced him to be President should his elder brother not return home from the War. His elder brother was killed when his airplane exploded by accident. She died in an airplane accident too, **starting** the *Kennedy Family Curse*. Writing was easy for him, that he earned awards from it. He also desired to return in a future life to overthrow the USSR (Russia) using Psychic Warfare (i.e. Egyptian Magic). Horus avenges the previous life of Asaris.

Chapter 5:

1

Tutankhamon was reincarnated into an American over in California on the exact same birthday of *Howard Carter*. This incarnation was **Michael**.

2

The soul of **AmonRa** impregnated the mother during intercourse but before any sperm had reached their target, as the father had said. The father was later confused as to why she became with child. He later separated because he was not ready to be a father.

3

At **age 3** Michael had a childhood accident with his babysitter, whereby his soul was detached and entered the Afterlife. He returned to his body and **resurrected**. The babysitter was perplexed by this and so she disappeared.

4

Michael's mother remarried, this time to an Englishman with **royal ancestry**. They moved to another city in California. His step-father is **related to many Kings**.

5

Michael was exposed to violence by new neighbors **from *Palestine***. This negatively influenced him in later years. Michael became a **Writer**, and wrote his first book while in high school. It was published by a **woman** who later told him was his babysitter **who saw him** resurrect at age 3.

6

The babysitter was named ***Karen***. When the book was in circulation the USA Government heard about it and investigated. Karen had taken a photocopy of it and published it herself without informing Michael of this, as a surprise. When he discovered this he was furious, but she came to his home with intent to kill him and keep the proceeds of the stolen book, which was in the Millions of Dollars. Michael did not go outside after hearing her **taunt** him. Instead he waited.

7

Karen was taken to a Mental Hospital and was heard screaming at the doctors. The USA Government confiscated the book and its proceeds, then they classified Michael top secret to prevent others from knowing about him. The **book** was a *new religion* now.

8

The book was written in supernatural energy, so the events in the book influenced real events after being read by the living. For example, the events about Arabic Terrorism (written in 1989) caused the *War on Islamic Terrorism* over 10 years later. The Palestinians influenced Michael's writings in this regard. The book itself **was fictional** at the time of authorship. This book fulfilled the role of **Christ.** It was called *Eye of the Pharaoh* ©1990. The 'eye' was the *Eye of Sacrifice*, as **the book was a sacrificial offering to Queen Ankhesenamon**, whom the book was dedicated to.

9

Michael was also a **Kheri-Heb Priest** of the Traditional Egyptian religion and an expert in Egyptian Magic. He summoned the Angels of Heaven to Earth, including the Angel of **Ankhesenamon**, one of his Guardian Angels. They protected him from danger and the Palestinians when they sought to strike him.

10

As a Kheri-Heb, Michael wielded much power. He could influence Earthquakes, Storms, Flash Floods, Erosion, and the Sun.

11

Michael used his powers to influence Politics by writing to the Government, as Jack Kennedy often did as a youth. He used his power to overthrow the USSR, conquer North Korea in 1994 by cursing their leaders, attack Middle Eastern Nations, inspired the Arab Spring Democracy Revolution of 2011 (via his book's prophecy), and cause Tsunamis in Indonesia the day *after* Christmas (Gods do not work on holidays) in 2004.

12

Michael became *King of the World* by conquering and influencing civilization; however this was a **secret** of the Government. The Palestinians sought to acquire his secrets after their leader was killed the year when Michael graduated from his University with a degree in Archaeology (1999). Michael was recognized as the *Sovereign Lord* in 1993 after he overthrew the USSR; this was a title of Pharaoh, *or God*. The title was made public.

13

The *Palestinians* **bribed the USA Government for information** about their neighbor. They then made all secret knowledge about Michael **public**.

14

The Palestinians are from the *House of Bread*, whose parents were from Arabic *Jerusalem*. They openly attacked Michael as by throwing rocks, later brandishing guns or making physical threats of violence to Michael or his family. Michael practiced his powers on *them* **first** *before* conquering the World.

15

Michael learned via public gossip (word of mouth) that he "owns an island" and other real estate on Earth, via the USA Government. Michael was informed about the proceeds of his stolen book were stored in the Government. So he told them to "buy things" with it, and this data was stolen by the Palestinians and was made public by them. Doing so amounts to Treason, and they were fined $10,000 for their crimes.

16

Michael told his neighbors the "island" was Niihau, a Hawaiian Island with a Military Base on it, so when they went there to spy on it, the USA Military became upset by the interlopers. The neighbors believed Niihau was a "new country," though they only saw the Base from a distance.

17

Michael governed the World with stories and characters from those stories interacted with real people, as Michael was a Writer. He used his first novel as a basis for these stories as it was becoming real by its own power.

18

Michael's stories contained a country mentioned by JESUS CHRIST as being the *Kingdom of God on Earth* - a new Egyptian nation. This nation was advertised by the USA Government since 1993, on television and other venues. It was the fulfillment of the Prophecy of Asaris, another Kingdom of Egypt, to be created once evil was vanquished. One element was the symbolic *Kingdom of Niihau*, founded on July 5, 2000 by "**Pharaoh M7.**" This country was also added to via Internet websites, books, and blogs.

19

Michael also wrote Magic books to express his power and thus help others. People would read these books and could heal the sick, cast out unclean spirits, raise the dead, or become prosperous just by using the books. This is a written form of *Christhood*.

Book 2: Netra (Prayers)

Chapter 1: (The Names of Asaris)

The *Sacred Names of Asaris* (Osiris) will work miracles when written or over time when uttered or spoken. **Repeat 10x** or as necessary per solar day. Also pray *during* a Full Moon, as Asaris was once a Moon God. *Praying to* the Sun or Moon *will influence actions on Earth.* The Moon controls the tides and atmosphere, while the Sun influences storms, weather, rain, and social conditions of humanity.

1

Asaris Unnefer:

Pray to Asaris Unnefer whenever you are lonely, need emotional support, or mental courage and strength. He also provides inspiration and protects the unborn.

2

Asaris Ankhi

Pray to Asaris Ankhi whenever you are in doubt or are unsure of yourself. He will lift the burden of hardship, and give strength and council.

3

Asaris Neb Ankh

Pray to Asaris Neb Ankh (*Lord of Life*) whenever you need to heal someone from all or any illness, cure diseases, or find a solution to a problem.

4

Asaris Nebertcher

Pray for provisions of Food and Drink, clothing, possessions and real estate. This name will attract all that you desire.

5

Asaris Apdjedtawi

Prayers will restore Justice to any Government, and calm any riots or conspiracies. Effective at night when there is Moonlight.

6

Asaris Khentet Un

Prayers will influence Government towards the benefit of society. Laws will be written with Fairness and Justice, not based on personal feelings or grievances.

7

Asaris Khentet Nepra

Prayers will protect Law Enforcement officers from rioters, anarchists, criminals, terrorists or the Mentally Unstable.

Asaris Saph

Prayers will straighten bent bones or vertebrae, nourish the body with rejuvenation or heal Pestilence.

Asaris Seps Baiu Annu

Prayers will summon to you Medical Professionals, Doctors, Nurses, or Dentists and other Specialists. It will also attract First Aid kits.

10

Asaris Khenti Thenenet

This Prayer will heal one's body using heated water, as in a Hot Tub. It will also protect you from Dehydration or Vitamin D deficiency by exposure to sunlight.

11

Asaris Em Resenet

Prayer will influence a Garden or Lotus Pool; it also will affect fields and attract a Good Harvest.

12

Asaris Em Mehenet

This Prayer assists Tailors, Blacksmiths, Merchants, and Shopkeepers. It will attract customers and expand businesses.

13

Asaris Neb Heh

This prayer will safeguard your tomb and your ancestor's tombs; it will provide sustenance for your Akh in the Afterlife, and protect your living heirs wherever they are.

14

Asaris Sa Erpeti

This Prayer protects Vineyards and Breweries from insects and mold. It also provides you with servants, on Earth *or* in the Afterlife.

15

Asaris Ptah Neb Ankh

This Prayer mixes the Technological Science of Asaris with the creative will of Ptah. It will solve complex problems and inspire you with visions and new ideas.

16

Asaris Khent-Restau

This Prayer protects the souls of the recent dead from going to *Aset Tchabet* (i.e. Hell). In turn they will become workers (**Shabtis**) in the fields of grain in the Domain of Asaris, unless noted elsewhere.

17

Asaris Heq taiu her-ab Tattu

This prayer cures drunkenness and will sober up anyone drunk *within 2 days.*

18

Asaris Her-ab Set

This Prayer relieves Depression and Heart diseases or Blood Pressure problems by calming the heart and mind.

19

Asaris Ba sheps em Tattu

This Prayer provides nourishment to the souls of the Afterlife, and to *your soul* while it lives within you, by giving you *Enlightenment* (Inspiration of ideas).

20

Asaris Em Atet

This Prayer will find any lost item within minutes. It will also give a vision of the object's location if it is not nearby.

21

Asaris Em Hest

This Prayer will bless people who have sinned, and consecrate the unborn with Powers. The blessing will remove all evil actions from their form so they won't fall into the Abyss upon death.

22

Asaris Neb ta ankhtet

This Prayer will provide Housing for a departed Soul or Spirit, in the Afterlife. The residence will come with furniture, an Offerings Chamber, a Chapel, a Granary with irrigated gardens, and a boat dock. Daily offerings will be made there by *Shabtis*.

23

Asaris Em Sau

This Prayer will protect your home and belongings, pets, job, and your neighbor's items while you are away or on vacation.

Asaris Em Netchet

This Prayer will protect your ancestors or your Tomb(s), gravesites, etc. from the Weather, from malicious people, or Erosion.

25

Asaris Em Resu

This Prayer will grant you a raise in pay at your occupation, or cause Prosperity for your businesses.

Asaris Em Pe

This Prayer introduces your Akh (*Angelic Form*) to the **City of Pe** in the Afterlife. It will also attract Grants or Scholarships to College students and Medical or Law students.

Asaris Em Tept

This Prayer will destroy all your enemies, if you have any. Otherwise it will cause the sky to rain or flood *for 3 weeks.*

28

Asaris Em Netra

This Prayer gives you Divine or Sacred Energy,
to perform healing and sexual ecstasy.

29

Asaris Em Sau Khert

This Prayer will fertilize the Fields for an
Excellent Harvest; or *Surplus Budget* in either a
company or a government.

30

Asaris Em Sau Hert

This Prayer will give good ratings on a Stock Exchange Market, or give excellent returns on a Casino slot machine, or help you win any contest, sweepstakes, exam, or situation.

31

Asaris Em An-rut-f

This Prayer will enable you to win in all Games of Chance, and win a *Jackpot Prize*. It will also *attract* Money to you *from afar*.

32

Asaris Em Bakui

If you are ever *defeated* by a situation or are frustrated by an event, this Prayer will make you *successful* and victorious over any situation.

33

Asaris Em Sunnu

When someone you know *dies*, this Prayer will comfort you and remove sorrow or despair.

34

Asaris Em Renen

This Prayer will attract to you: **friends** (*or lovers*) or people who are or may become important in life.

35

Asaris Em Aper

This Prayer will *counter-attack* a hidden Enemy with supernatural energy, and whoever is cursing you with it.

36

Asaris Em Qefennu

This Prayer causes *Natural Disasters* to an Enemy, such as *random* Earthquakes, Storms, Flash Floods, or Erosion.

37

Asaris Em Sekri

This Prayer will summon *Spirits* (or souls) of the Dead to you, to be used as Guardian or Protective *Angels* (Akhu).

38

Asaris Em Petet

This Prayer will send a **Good soul** *directly to Heaven* after transition.

39

Asaris Em Hetef Em Restau

This Prayer sends any soul or spirit to *Purgatory*, which is the **first level of the Afterlife** before visiting the Court of Asaris (for *Judgement of the Soul*).

40

Asaris Em Nifur

This Prayer will increase the regularity of *breathing*, or relieve shortness of breath. It will also give the *Breath of Life* for healing.

41

Asaris Em Netit

This Prayer **stops** all fighting, arguments, battles, etc. with a *Peace Treaty* or *Ceasefire*. It will also rarely cause *World Peace* for 24 hours.

42

Asaris Khenti Nutef

This Prayer will fertilize fields or assist ranchers and farmers. It also protects crops during a storm or other weather.

43

Asaris Henti

This Prayer *summons* to you books, Compact Disks or Laser Disks, and knowledge. It is useful for inspiration *or Enlightenment.*

44

Asaris Em Pekes

This Prayer helps with sexual conditions, infertility or Menstruation. It also protects the unborn and assists with delivery.

45

Asaris Em Hetef am ta reset

This Prayer will attract real estate or properties to you, and make significant discounts on purchases.

46

Asaris Em hetef am ta mehet

Prayers will protect animals from becoming road-kill or from accidents.

47

Asaris Em Pet

This Prayer will cause you or someone else to be *remembered* (by name) *in Heaven and Duat.*

48

Asaris Em ta

This Prayer *will undo any Magic*, whether it is a Spell or a Curse, Enchantment, or evil energy.

49

Asaris Em Nest

This Prayer *repels* Criminals, Hostile People, feral animals, dangerous or poisonous insects or plants, and helps alleviate sting bites.

50

Asaris Em Atef-ur

This Prayer is a *Protection* against *any evil* who wishes to attack or influence you or your family, friends, associates or group.

51

Asaris Sokar em Shetat

This Prayer will *attract* riches, wealth, prosperity, or *influence* Lotteries and other Games to one's benefit.

Asaris heq tchetta em Annu

This Prayer will cause you to *avoid contact with* people who leave *negative reviews* of your products, like with *Internet Trolls & Flamers*, or other hostile or unfriendly people.

53

Asaris Utet

This Prayer replenishes *sexual energy* and *vigor*, with new energy.

54

Asaris Em Sektet

This Prayer *attracts transportation* vehicles to you, as when you are stranded or need a ride somewhere.

55

Asaris Em Rertu-nifu

This Prayer will bring the *Winds of Change* into your life, replaces despair with hope and tranquility.

56

Asaris Neb-tchetta

This Prayer will render you *invisible or hidden*
to danger, or to any enemy.

57

Asaris Neb-Heh

This Prayer will influence the Future to your
benefit, or resolve any situation with wisdom
and thoughtfulness.

58

Asaris Em Tesher

This Prayer *will bring Rain* and reduce a Drought with increased rain. It will also cause *or stop* a Flood.

59

Asaris Em Seshet

This Prayer *protects children* from bullies, and from becoming bullies *if abused by bullies*.

60

Asaris Em Utet-resu

This Prayer will purify the air by attracting cleanliness and purity, as with incense, Natron, fog or soap.

61

Asaris Em Utet-Mehet

This Prayer *will capture or vanquish* Terrorists, Arsonists, Vandals, Rioters, and other criminal persons from one's vicinity.

62

Asaris Em Aat-urt

This Prayer will *vindicate **or liberate** you or your associates from any litigation* in Court, and find evidence in support of this.

63

Asaris Em Apert

This Prayer *will heal the sick* and cast out "unclean spirits" that cause diseases or misfortune.

64

Asaris Em Shennu

This Prayer will protect your home and possessions while you are traveling, and those of your friends or extended family and pets.

65

Asaris Em Hekennut

This Prayer *will bind an enemy sorcerer* in a triangle and prevent their actions from attacking you, your family and friends, or city, county, or country.

66

Asaris Em Sokar

This Prayer will *counter-attack an enemy* with Frost and Fire, or make them have nausea, dizziness, or chills and a fever.

67

Asaris Em Shau

This Prayer will immediately **stop** any Earthquakes or redirect Storms away from you or a target.

68

Asaris Fa-Horu

This Prayer will attract *or allow one to obtain* excellent **employment** with good benefits.

69

Asaris Em Uu-Pek

This Prayer *attracts to you* gold and silver coins or bullion, hidden treasures, and shipwrecks, hoards, or gems.

70

Asaris Em Maati

This Prayer will find the truth in all matters.

71

Asaris Em Mena

This Prayer will cause Good Luck.

72

Asaris Baiu-tef-f

This Prayer will exorcise, clean, or purge a place or person from hostile or unclean spirits, demons, devils, foreign sorcery, Evil or Magic.

Book 3: Hekau (Magic):

Invocation (Spoken) Spells:

Chapter 1: Protection

To Protect someone from whatever obstacles are in the way; to Protect from hidden dangers:

DUA NAKHT HORUR DI WADJET ANKH

To Protect from all adversaries, whether hidden or visible:

DUA HORUR AA DI WADJET ANKH ES NEFRU

To Summon Soldiers, Police, Security Guards and Medical people:

 DUA NEITH AA MONTU AA HORUR DI ANKH

To Summon an Army:

DUA SHABTIS-XA HORUR SET DI ANKH

To Protect your home and possessions while traveling:

DUA SELQET NEPHTHYS BES BAST DI ANKH

To Protect your city:

DUA IPET-ISUT AMONRA NEITH DI ANKH

To Protect Egypt from harm or evil:

DUA KMT PTAH-TANNEN HORUR DI ANKH

To Protect USA (America) from harm or evil:

DUA NEITH SELQET AMON SET DI ANKH

To Protect a region from harm or evil:

DUA NOMES DI ANKH HOTEPU

To Protect you while practicing Magic:

DUA HEKAU NETRA THOTH ZEHUTY DI ANKH

For Protection in general:

DUA SEREKH REN HORUR MICHAEL DI ANKH

For Protection while having surgery:

DUA ZEHUTY IMHOTEP DI ANKH HOTEPU

For Protection during any Medical or Dental treatment:

DUA ZEHUTY SESHET SELQET DUAMUTEF

For Protection from Liars and Deception:

DUA MAAT MAATI ASARIS EM HOTEP

For Protection from sales people or unwanted Charities:

DUA ASARIS HOTEP DI ANKH HOTEPU

For Protection while operating a vehicle:

DUA WERRET AMONRA DI ANKH WADJET

For Protection while driving a Car or Boat:

DUA WERRET EN NETER DI ANKH HOTEPU

For Protection from insects:

DUA SELQET BES ANKH

For Protection from Animals (Feral or Domestic):

DUA BAST ANUP HATHOR SOBEK ANKH

For Protection from Stings:

DUA BITY SELQET NEITH ANKH DI URP

For Protection from Birds or Lizards:

DUA ZEHUTY RA HORUR DI ANKH

For Protection from shellfish or aquatic beings:

DUA SOBEK KHAT NU ANKH DI HOTEPU

For Protection from Snakes & Serpents:

DUA SET ANKH NI APOPHIS

For Protection from Viruses:

DUA HORUR AA DI ANKH

For Protection from Misfortune:

DUA KHEPERI SHAI NEFERU DI MAAT

For Protection from the Weather:

DUA AMONRA AMONKA PTAH ANKH

For Protection from unclean Spirits:

DUA IESUS ASARIS EM HOTEP DI ANKH

For Protection from any illness or disease:

AR NEFRU SONEB DI MAAT ANKH ES NEFRU

For Protection from contagious illnesses:

DUA THOTH IMHOTEP SELQET ANKH

To Protect against unseen issues:

DUA AMON DI ANKH NEBA

For Spiritual Purification:

DUA AB-EN NEFRU AKH

To cleanse a Soul from evil:

AR AB-EN NEFERU AKH DI ANKH

To become hidden, "invisible:"

DUA AMON NEB-RA

For Emergencies Only:

DUA WADJET ANKH PERT-KHERT MAAXORU

For Protection from Internet Crimes:

DUA THOTH PTAH TANNEN ANKH

For Protection from unstable People:

DUA ANUBIS DI MAAT ANKH NEFRU

For Protection from Enemies:

DUA HORUR MAAT GEB NI ISFET

For Protection from Riots, Anarchy:

DUA MAAT PERAA ASARIS ANKH

For Protection from *all forms of* Terrorism or Harassment or Assault:

DUA PERAA HORUR MAAXORU ANKH

To Protect from symptoms of Mental Illness:

DUA ZEHUTY NETRA IESUS NEITH DI ANKH HOTEPU URP-NEFERU

For Protection from Cancers or Burns:

DUA SAKHMET RA NI UBETET-XA

To Protect your Occupation or Job:

DUA PER-ANKH DI MAAT DJED SA ANKH

To Protect your Home, Pets, belongings:

DUA BASTET BES NEKHEN NEITH NEPHTHYS ANKH EM HOTEP MAAXORU

To Protect your Family:

DUA MAHIU ANKH DI ANKH SA

To Protect Friends and Associates:

DUA HORUR SESHEN BES ANKH

To Protect Gardens:

DUA HAPY NU SHU AMON RA ANKH HOTEP

To Protect against Black Mold:

DUA SHU AMON ANKH

To Protect Children:

DUA BES NEITH DI ANKH

To Protect the Unborn:

DUA BES SHAI NEFERU

To Protect Children from Bullies:

DUA BES NI SET

For Protection from Droughts:

DUA TEFNUT AA

For Protection from Fear, have Courage:

AR MAAXORU

For Protection from Excessive Weather (Rain, storms, blizzards, etc.):

DUA TEFNUT ANKH PERT-KHERU HOTEP

For Protection from Air Turbulence:

DUA HORU MAAXORU

For Protection from Fires or Electrical problems:

DUA SAKHMET RA HOTEP

For Protection from Gas Explosions:

DUA SHU HOTEP DI ANKH PGE

For Protection from Vandalism:

DUA HORUR NEITH ISIS BES ANKH

To bind enemy Sorcerers in a Triangle to prevent their actions from success:

AR HEKAU-ISFET NI MAAXORU ANKH

To bind enemy Demons or Evil Spirits in a Triangle to prevent actions by them:

AR KAU SEBA NI MAAXORU ANKH

To bind Devils in a triangle to prevent actions:

AR SET APOPHIS SEBA NI MAAXORU ANKH

To render enemy Magic useless and powerless to cause an effect:

DUA HORUR MICHAEL MAAXORU DI ANKH URP

To Protect one's Army:

DUA MONTU AMON SA ANKHU NU MENTIT XA

To Protect from hostile or negative Magical Energy:

DUA NEFERTUM SA SAKHMET DI ANKH

To bless those cursed with negative Energy:

DUA SAKHEM-NEFERU DI ANKH MAAXORU

To build a Wall of Protective Barrier Energy:

AR SENEB S-NAKHT EM SAKHEM KA

To protect your names:

AR SA REN DI ANKH MAAXORU

To protect animals and other life:

DUA ANKH DI ANKH SA

To undo any Magic cast by you:

AR HEKAU NI MAAXORU

To undo any *other* Magic:

AR NETRA NI MAAXORU

To undo a Curse:

AR SET HEKAU NI MAAXORU

To remove Enchantment:

AR PERT-HORU NI MAAXORU

For Divine Protection (by Angels):

DUA AKHU-NEFRU ANKH

To Protect Tombs & Gravesites:

DUA ASARIS PER-SHEN ANKH DI SA

For protection from Computer-based criminals or hackers:

DUA SOBEK AA NEITH ANKH

For Protection from Cyber-crimes:

DUA PTAH TANNEN NI ISEFET

For Protection from Internet Warfare:

DUA MONTU SET APOPHIS NI ISFET

For Protection from Computer problems:

SA MEDAT ANKH

To protect you when reading ancient documents:

BU AB-EN BU AA MI AMONRA SHEN

For protection from Food Poisoning:

AR HEBET ANKH NI MENU

To protect anyone from Misfortune:

DUA WADJET EM HOTEP NEFRU

For protection from the "Evil Eye":

DUA WADJET NEFRU SA ANKH

To Liberate from imprisonment:

AR MAAT MAAXORU DI MAATI

For acquiring protective amulets or charms:

AR HEKAU ANKH DJED WADJET UAS XA

For protection from unwanted negative reviews on your products:

AR NEFRU MRY NI ISFET

For a Magic Circle:

AR SHEN DI REN

For protection from tree, animal or bird droppings:

AR KHEPERI SA NI ANEF

For Protection from astral assaults from enemy body parts occurring in the astral plane:

DUA TUTANKHAMIN ANKH NI ISFET

For protection from skin diseases:

DUA MAAT NI WASHESH

To Protect the Dead & Undead:

DUA ASARIS DI ANKH SENTRA URP HOTEPU

Chapter 2: Politics

To secure a Country's Borders:

AR SENEB S-NEHI S-NEKHT XA AMON

To prevent spies from stealing secrets:

AR SENEB SBAI HORU NI R-DIAST MEDIT XA

To prevent hackers from stealing data:

DUA NEBKHEPERURA KA-NAKHT TUT-MESU

To collect revenue from taxes or tariffs:

DUA ASARIS DI KHERIT XA

To reduce tax amounts:

AR KHERI-A NI XA

To resolve Homelessness:

DUA PERAA DI PER-ANKH EM ANKHU

To feed the hungry and destitute:

DUA ANKHU DI PERT-KHERU XA

To encourage foreign economies:

AR SHUI-T UPI HAU KHERT EM SETHIU XA

To create jobs for the Poor:

AR UPI DUA AMONRA NEB-NUB

To clothe those without money:

AR SENDYT I'AW XA PERT-KHERU

To medicate Mentally Ill people:

AR NEFER-TAP NERAU PEKHAR-T XA

To fund Education of the people:

AR NUB EN KHERI-A SBAI XA

To care for the Disabled & Elderly:

AR NUB XA EM SHAKER ANKH IK

To fund Scientific Research:

AR KHERIT EM TEP AMI-AST-A DUA THOTH

To fund Medicine Research:

AR KHERIT EM TEP NERAU DUA SESHET

To fund Military Technology Research:

AR KHERIT EM TEP S-NEHEP XA DUA AMON

To increase (decrease) Weapons Technology:

AR S-NEHEP S-NEKHET (NI DI KHEPESH)

To adhere to written legislation:

DUA MAAT ASARIS DI MAAT

To make new Laws:

AR MAAT XA

To compel Citizens to obey Laws:

DUA ASARIS MAAT ANUBIS DI ANKH URP

For Justice:

DUA MAAT MAATI DI ANKH MAAXORU

For Truth in Justice:

AR MAAT DUA MAAT MAAXORU

For Law & Order in society:

AR MAAT EM ANKH KMT

To prevent all or any Crimes:

DUA ANKHU HIYZESN NEFERU DI MAAT

To prevent Terrorism:

DUA HORUR PERT-KHERU NI ISFET

To prevent Anarchy & Riots:

DUA ANKHU ANKH NEFRU NI ISFET XA

To quell riots and anti-Government groups:

DUA HORUR ANKHU ANKH NI ISFET XA

To arrest malicious vandals, Internet hackers, arsonists, thugs, rogues, bullies, assailants, thieves, brigands, pirates, Internet Trolls and Flamers, blasphemers, heretics, and other violators of Laws:

AR MAAT MID PTAH ASARIS RA ANKH

To capture murderers, vandals, arsonists, thieves, terrorists, and other wanted violators of Laws:

AR MAAT DI MAAT DUA MAAT RA ANKH

To prevent or stop Sexual Crimes:

AR MAAT DUA HATHOR MIN NI MES KHEBNT

To prevent over-medication (drug abuse):

AR SONEB-NEFRU NI DI NERAU XA

To write Just and Fair Legislation (Laws):

AR MAAT TEP NEFERU MAAXORU

To prevent Wars or Battles:

AR HOTEP EM ANKHU

To strengthen one's Military:

AR S-NEKHT ANKH-NU-MENTIT XA

To enlist new soldiers:

AR S-NEHEP XA DUA MONTU AMON

To cause a battle or war:

DUA SET MONTU AMON DI S-NEHI XA

To stop a battle or war (Cease-fire):

DUA ASARIS NEB-PAX HOTEP MAAXORU

To order Tribute from a defeated foe:

DUA HORU DI THES EM S-NEHET XA

To safeguard Artwork during War:

DUA PTAH KHNUM DI PER-ANKH IKET XA

To prevent War Crimes during War:

DUA PTAH MAAT KA NI KHEBNIT SET

To conquer a rogue State:

AR S-NERIT TAU KHEFA KHEFTI XA

To overthrow a regime:

AR TAU SENIB SENA S-NEHET XA DUA HORU

To create well-paying jobs for the people:

AR KHERT DI NUB HEH

To cause a Budget Surplus:

AR SHAKER HEH EM KHERIT ANKH

For Happiness in general:

AR ANKHU NEFERU EM HOTEP

For Prosperity:

AR NUB HEDA HEH DUA AMONRA

For Long Life of citizens:

AR ANKH SHEN SONEB NEFRU

For a Good Harvest:

AR SHUI-T NEFERU HEH DI SHAI NEFERU

For healthy Citizens:

AR SONEB-NEFRU ANKH XA

For healthy Food & social customs:

AR SONEB-NEFERU PESIT ARP TA

For Affordable Medicine/Care:

AR SONEB-NEFERU DI NUB ANKH

To prevent Sorcerers from operating:

DUA SET NI HEKAU MAAXORU

To reduce crime in cities:

DUA MENNOFER MAAT NI KHEBNIT

For increased exports revenue

AR KHERI-A HEH DI ANKH HOTEPU

To stop Mayhem or Civil Strife:

DUA AMONRA OSIRIS DI MAAT

To stop wildfires and accidents:

DUA SAKHMET DI HOTEP

For people to be Good and Safe:

AR ANKH BU NEFERU SA XA

To Protect Law Enforcement:

AR NAKHT HEM MAAT ANKHU DI SA

To Protect Civil Servants:

AR SA ANKHU DI MAAT MAAXORU

To Protect the Military Folk:

AR SA ANKHU NU MENTIT XA

Chapter 3: War (Red) Magic

To seize one's enemy's powers and energy:

AR MAAT DI HEKAU SAKHEM

To be hidden from an Enemy:

DUA AMON DUA ATONRA DI MAAXORU

To counter an attack by an Enemy:

DUA SET HORUR MONTU DI ANKH MAAT

To counter any Challenge:

DUA SET NEITH SELQET DI PERT KHERU

To undo any Enemy Magic:

AR HEKAU KHEBNIT NI MAAXORU

To melt an unruly soul in the Abyss:

DUA ASARIS NEB-ANKH NEB-NEBU SHEN

To counter-attack with Frost & Fire:

DUA SHU TEFNUT DI MAAXORU URP XA

To undo Military Magic:

AR BU ABEN MI AMONRA MONTU HEH

For justified revenge against an Enemy:

DUA HORU SET DI MAAT MAAXORU XA

For capturing a routed Enemy Army:

AR ANKH DI SNA PETCHI XA

For destroying Enemy Strongholds, bases and sanctuaries:

AR KHEFA AQHAU XA SENIB DI MAAXORU

For disorder in Enemy leadership:

AR TEP EN SNA DI ISFET NI MAAXORU

To destroy an Enemy Army:

AR SNA PETCHI SENIB DUA HORUR DI ANKH

To "Kill" Enemy Soldiers, Terrorists:

AR SNA PETCHI DI MUT

To cause an Enemy to be Fatigued, tired:

AR SNA NI KAU

To train soldiers for battle:

AR S-NEHEP S-NEHI XA DUA AMON

To plunder an Enemy's Treasury:

AR SNA KHEFA NUB HEH

To cause an Enemy to have medical or health problems and issues:

AR SNA NI SONEB NEFERU

To cause an Enemy *Army* to have medical or health problems and issues:

AR SNA XA NI SOBEB NEFERU

To cause an Enemy base to be surrounded and defenseless:

AR SNA SENIB NI MAAXORU HEH

To *confuse* an Enemy (Sent Evil Spirits or Demons) to become confused on orders issued against their target:

DUA SET DUA HORUR DI ANKH NI SNA SA

To rain down fire and sulfur upon an Enemy Army:

DUA TEFNUT SAKHMET NI SNA XA PETTIU

To attack an Enemy Navy at Sea:

DUA HAPY NU SAKHMET SHU DI ANKH

To attack an Enemy with Thieves:

AR SNA DI AUAU XA NI SA

For an Enemy to be defeated:

AR SNA XA NI MAAXORU

For Arabic Terrorists to be defeated:

AR SNA ARAM XA DI SUKKA NI MAAXORU

For an Enemy to be in a riot, argument:

AR SNA DI BAGASA

To rain down Frogs & Locusts onto an Enemy:

AR SNA DI ABNEKA XA SANHEM XA

To cause a Flood to an Enemy:

AR SNA DI AGAB

To cause an Enemy to have cysts:

AR SNA DI NEHP-T XA

To cause an Enemy to have Fires:

AR SNA DI HEM TAU

To know that I am not your Enemy and therefore cannot be attacked by you using my Magic Books:

DUA HORUR MICHAEL DI ANKH PERT-KHERU

To forgive your Enemy and to forgive those who trespass against us:

DUA IESUS KRST AMONRA DI ANKH HOTEP

To 'turn the other cheek' / look the other way:

DUA KHONSU TEP DI ANKH HOTEPU URP NEFRU EM HOTEP MAAXORU

For an Enemy to have Sanctuary for healing wounds or to confess of their sins:

DUA AMONRA NEB-MRY NEB-ANKH DI ANKH

For an Enemy to surrender to the Righteous:

AR SNA DI MAAT NI ISFET, DUA HORUR ANKH

For Mercy from an Enemy:

AR SNA DI MRY MAAT EM HOTEP NI ISIS HOTEP

For Compassion to an Enemy:

DUA MRYT-MIN MRYT-HATHOR NI SNA XA

To Conquer an Enemy:

AR S-NERIT SNA XA DUA HORUR ANKH HOTEP

To overthrow a Corrupt Government:

AR SENB SENA TAU PER-AA NI SEBA ANKH

Chapter 4: Weather (Elemental)

To cause Rain:

HAIL TEFNUT, GODDESS OF MOISTURE!

To cause Morning Dew or Humidity:

HAIL TEFNUT AND SHU, THE DIVINE TWINS!

To cause Snow:

HAIL TEFNUT, COLD OF WINTER!

To cause Wind Gusts:

HAIL AMUN AND SHU, GIVEN OFFERINGS!

To cause a Clear Sky with Sunshine:

HAIL RA, THE GREAT SOLAR GOD!

To cause a Rainbow:

HAIL AMONRA TEFNUT AND SHU!

To cause overcast Clouds:

HAIL TEFNUT, LADY OF GRAY!

To cause the Sun to open in the sky:

HAIL PTAH, THE OPENER OF WAYS!

To cause Floods:

HAIL TEFNUT, YOUR CHILD HAS RED HAIR!

To make peace with the Gods:

HAIL THE NETERU (NETJERU), GIVEN OFFERINGS!

To undo any Magic:

HAIL HORUS-MICHAEL, GOD OF WEALTH!

To cause the sky to rain down Frogs:

HAIL HEKET, THE FROG GODDESS!

For Silence in the Sky:

HAIL HARPOCRATES FOREVER!

For a Solar Heat wave:

HAIL AMONRA AND SHU FOREVER!

For mild weather:

HAIL RA TEFNUT HORUS, GIVEN OFFERINGS!

To Stop Erosion:

HAIL GEB AND TEFNUT FOREVER!

For clear-air turbulence:

DUA SHU AA AMON AA

To stop clear-air turbulence

DUA SHU AMON NI AA DI HOTEP

To cause Rain:

DUA TEFNUT DI HOTEPU ANKH

To cause Floods:

DUA TEFNUT SA SET DI ANKH

To cause Wind:

DUA AMUN DI ANKH

To cause Sunshine in the Clouds:

DUA RA ATON NI APOPHIS

To cause a Rainbow:

DUA AR TEFNUT SA HORU

To cause Moisture, Humidity or Dew:

DUA TEFNUT AA

To cause High Tides:

DUA KHONSU NUNU

To cause Erosion from Weather:

SA GEB DUA TEFNUT AA

To cause Sinkholes:

DUA GEB TEFNUT DI ANKH

To cause Mudslides:

DUA GEB AA TEFNUT AA

To cause an Avalanche:

DUA SET HORU AA DI ANKH

To cause small Earthquakes or Tremors:

DUA GEB AA

To cause a Tsunami (Tidal Wave):

DUA GEB AA NUNU

To cause Tornadoes (Vortex):

DUA AMUN AA

To cause Hurricanes, Typhoons:

DUA AMUN SET DI HOTEPU

To cause Volcanoes to erupt:

DUA SET GEB PELE AA

To cause Warm Air or Weather:

DUA SHU AA

To cause Hail:

DUA SHU TEFNUT AA DI ANKH

To cause Snow:

DUA AMUN TEFNUT SET AA

To cause Blizzards:

SA HORUR DUA TEFNUT SET AA

To cause Strong Winds (Turbulence):

SA HORU DUA SHU AMUN AA

To cause the Winds to stop:

SA HORU DUA AMUN HOTEP

To cause the Rains to stop:

SA HORU DUA TEFNUT QRST HOTEP

To cause Earthquakes to Stop:

SA GEB DUA SET HOTEP

To cause Wildfires:

SA GEB DUA SAKHMET AA

To cause Wildfires to Stop:

DUA SAKHMET HOTEP DI ANKH

To stop the effects of Drought or Famine:

SA GEB NUNU DUA TEFNUT AA

To cause dryness:

SA AMUN DUA SHU AA

To cause Pestilence (Diseases):

DUA SAKHMET AA

To End Pestilence (End Diseases):

DUA SAKHMET HOTEP SA ANKHU

To cause Acid Rain:

DUA SET TEFNUT AA

To cause Darkness (Non-Eclipse):

DUA APOPHIS SA ANKH

To cause Overcast Clouds:

DUA APOPHIS HOTEP

To cause Low Tides:

DUA KHONSU HOTEP

To cause a Blood Moon:

DUA KHONSU SET AA

To cause a Comet (to appear):

DUA SHU GEB AA DI ANKH

To cause a Meteor (Etc.) to appear:

DUA NUT AA

To cause a Sandstorm:

DUA SAKHMET SET DI ANKH

To cause Dust storms:

DUA SET SHU AA

To cause a Waterspout:

DUA SHU NUNU AMUN AA

To fold back movement of Waters:

DUA MOSES KHERIHEB AA

To control Water and Air:

PU TEFNUT PU SHU DI ANKH

To cause Solar Flames:

DUA ATONRA SAKHMET AA

To evaporate rain water:

DUA ATONRA NI TEFNUT

To cause a Rain of Frogs (Seasonal):

DUA HEQET DI ANKH HOTEPU

To cause a Rain of Locusts:

DUA HORU SHU SELQET AA

To cause Boils (Cysts) on People or Cattle:

DUA SET AA NI SHU

To cause Lice or Fleas to appear:

SA ANKHU DUA KHEPERI

To undo all Weather Magic Now:

SA ANKH DI MAAXORU HOTEP

To cause a plague of Bees or Wasps:

SA BITY DUA SHU AA

For Fog:

SA TEFNUT DI ANKH URP-TAU

For Clouds:

SA SHU AMUN DI ANKH URP-TA

For Sunburn:

SA RA-ATON DI RA-ATON AA

To cause Thunder & Lightning:

DUA ZEUS THOR AMONRA SET DI ANKH URP

To cause Dry Lightning:

DUA ZEUS AMONRA SET SHU DI ANKH URP

To cause Hot Hail (from Volcano):

DUA GEB SHU TEFNUT DI ANKH URP NEFRU

Chapter 5: Wealth Spells

For one's book or music to be a Best Seller:

DUA THOTH AMUNRA HEH-HEH SHEN

For General Economic Prosperity:

DUA AMONRA DEDUN RENENUTET DI ANKH DI HOTEPU HEH

For acquiring Gold or Silver Coins or Ingots, or Antique Treasures:

DUA NUB NUBSENU MONETA AMONRA DI ANKH HOTEPU MAAT HEH HOTEP

For earning points on the Stock Market (NYSE, NASDAQ, etc):

DUA SESHET OSIRIS SESHU DI ANKH MAAT

For acquiring entitlements (Disability, Social Security, or other Benefits):

DUA SESHET THOTH POR-THRW DI ANKH

For new excessive earnings on investments:

DUA THOTH SESHET AMONRA DI ANKH

For acquiring rare antiques, stamps, artifacts, geo-facts, precious metals, old coins or currency, etc:

DUA NUBSENU SESHU AMONRA DI ANKH HOTEPU MAAT HOTEP

For excellent royalties on products, such as books or music:

DUA SESHET THOTH NUBSENU HEH DI ANKH DI MAAT DI HOTEPU HEH HOTEP

To be a Best-Selling Author for 1 month:

DUA AMONRA PTAH SESHET NUBSENU HEH DI ANKH DI MAATI DI HOTEPU XA HOTEP

To be Successful in any Endeavor:

DUA PTAH RA AMONRA MAAXERU HEH DI ANKH DI MAAT DI HOTEPU NUB SHEN

To win big in Gambling, Horse Races, Slot Machines, State or Inter-state Lotteries, Games, exams, tests, dice, drawings, etc., to win a "Jackpot":

DUA AMONRA AMONKA DI ANKH HEH

To acquire Seasonal Employment or Temporary work:

DUA SESHET THOTH DEDUN DI ANKH

To acquire steady modest employment with benefits:

DUA SESHET NEKHA HEH MONETA DI ANKH DI HOTEPU DI MAAT

To acquire excellent work with a high-paying salary and benefits:

DUA THOTH HEH MAAT DI ANKH URP PER-THRW HOTEPU HOTEP

For acquiring Free Money, Donations, Grants or Scholarships:

DUA NUBSENU MONETA PAX XA DI ANKH

To protect against peddlers, scams, salesmen, or high-pressure sales representatives:

DUA NEKHA NUBSENU NEHEBUKAU DI ANKH DI MAATI DI HOTEPU HOTEP

For protection from abusive Charities:

DUA NEKHA WERETHEKAU OSIRIS DI ANKH

To attract decent Charities, and to avoid crooked people:

DUA BES NEKHA NUBSENU HOTEP DI ANKH HOTEPU

For finding Money on the Ground:

DUA NUBSENU DI MONETA EM TA HOTEP

To attract Wealth:

DUA AMONRA AMONKA HEH HOTEP

To acquire *Endless* Wealth:

DUA AMONRA AKHU NEFRU DI HEH MONETA HEH SHEN

To become Translucent:

DUA AMUN HORU NUT RA DI ANKH!

To acquire Money (legally):

HAIL AMONRA FOREVER!

To acquire Money (donation):

HAIL THE RAM OF AMON FOREVER!

For excellent Stock Market Results:

HAIL THE BULL OF AMONRA FOREVER!

For winning in Games of Chance:

HAIL SHAI AMONRA, GODS OF FATE!

For winning an Interstate Lottery or Contest:

HAIL SHAI, GODDESS OF FATE, MAY I BE SUCCESSFUL IN THIS EXAM!

To acquire an excellent Job (employment) with Benefits:

HAIL AMONRA SESHET THOTH FOREVER!

To Excel in any Exam or Test:

HAIL SHAI, TRUE-OF-VOICE, FOREVER!

To win a contest or (Legal) Battle:

I AM TRUE-OF-VOICE, FOREVER!

To find and acquire hidden Treasures:

HAIL AMONRA, GOD OF WEALTH!

To find and acquire Golden coins or ingots:

HAIL HORUS-OF-GOLD, FOREVER!

To find Silver Money (attraction):

HAIL OSIRIS-OF-THE-MOON, FOREVER!

To find any missing or misplaced items:

HAIL THOTH THE THRICE-GREAT FOREVER!

To acquire State Entitlements (i.e. Welfare, etc.):

HAIL AMONRA, GOD OF MONETA-HEH!

To acquire Millions of whole currency:

HAIL AMONRA HEH NUBSENU FOREVER!

To become a Millionaire:

HAIL AMONRA HEH, GOD OF MILLIONS!

To double one's earnings (i.e. Promotion):

HAIL AMONRA SHAI HEH FOREVER!

To win in a Casino (i.e. in Slot Machines):

HAIL SHAI HEH AMON, GIVEN OFFERINGS!

To be Successful:

DUA MAAXORU EM HOTEP DI ANKH SHEN

To be a "Money Magnet" (attraction):

DUA AMON DI MONETA HEH DI ANKH HOTEPU

To seize money from the so-called Caliphate:

DUA AMONRA ANKH DI MONETA ISIS HEH

To destroy the Caliphate's Funding:

DUA AMONRA MONTU DI ANKH NI ISIS HEH

To form a Financial LLC/Incorporation:

DUA AMONRA DI ANKH DI MONETA HEH AA

For Gaming Credits, Chips, Stamps, etc.:

DUA AMONRA AMONKA DI ANKH HOTEPU

To find a shipwreck or gold/silver Mine:

DUA AMONRA DI NUB HEH AA ANKH

To find expensive artwork or ancient artifacts:

DUA NU NUT GEB OSIRIS DI ANKH

To become wealthy:

DUA AMONRA AMONKA MAAXORU DI ANKH NEB TAU MAAXORU HEH

For Success:

DUA KA MAAXORU HOTEP

To become a Billionaire:

DUA HEH SHAI AMONRA-M7 PTAH EM HOTEP

For a successful business merge or incorporation:

DUA SHAI SHESHET THOTH AMONRA DI HOTEP

To win in a drawing, contest or sweepstakes:

DUA SHAI AMONRA HORUR DI ANKH HOTEPU

To acquire a Business:

DUA PER-ANKH THOTH SESHAT HEH DI ANKH

Chapter 6: Healing Spells

For Excellent Health and Well-Being:

DUA IMHOTEP DI-NEFERU-SONEB

To cure or cease common cold or Influenza viruses, or other Pestilences:

DUA SAKHMET ANKH

To heal stomach flu, indigestion, diarrhea, constipation or pain:

DUA DUAMUTEF NEITH ANKH

To treat liver, gall or spleen conditions:

DUA AMSETI ISIS ANKH

To heal a cough, (breathing) or congestion:

DUA HAPY NEPHTHYS ANKH

To heal colon or intestinal issues or pain:

DUA QEBEHSENWF SELQET ANKH

To cure any infection or injury:

DUA NEHMETAWY ISHTAR

To heal heart conditions or heal Cancer:

DUA KHEPERI ANKH

To repair bones, cells, tissues, fractures or heal sprained tendons:

DUA THOTH IMHOTEP DJED

To rejuvenate one's health:

DUA HARPOCRATES SONEB-NEFRU ARQU

To heal back injuries or alleviate pain:

DUA THOTH DJED-NEFRU SIA

To alleviate Depression or Sadness:

DUA BES IHY OSIRIS HORI-SA-UR

For a safe childbirth:

DUA BES LAT BAST MESKHENET TAURET

To cure dehydration, heat stroke or dry skin:

DUA AB-NUNU MERIT MU ANKH

To restore (resurrect) an **intact body** with its original soul and spirit (**if it is willing**):

DUA PTAH-OSIRIS-RA WADJET WEPWAWET ANKH-SHEN

[Uses Telepathy + Chronokinesis]

To stop any addictions:

DUA WERETHEKAU IMHOTEP ANKH

To heal acute blindness or other discomfort:

DUA WADJET SIA SHAI NEFERU-SONEB

For increased Fertility, sexual energy:

DUA HATHOR MIN QETESH BAST

For better performance (sexual energy):

DUA QETESH HEQET BABI MIN

For attraction of a Mate or Lover:

DUA HATHOR MIN BAST

To cure common Pestilence:

DUA THOTH SAKHMET

To cure bacterial infections or parasites:

DUA NEHMETAWY SAKHMET BES

For increased bravery or courage:

DUA HORUR BABI MEH-URIT NEFERTUM

For invisibility, illusion (*works at right-angles*):

DUA AMUN WADJET SIA

To relieve skin conditions, acne, blemishes:

DUA ISHTAR ARQU IMHOTEP SONEB-ANKH

To relieve bodily pains, headaches, or cramps:

DUA MAAT SIA IMHOTEP NEKHA

To control blood cells in healing an injury or repel a bacterial infection:

DUA UKHET-ET THOTH SENIB ARQU

To cure **or** relieve symptoms of Cancer:

DUA SAKHMET RA HOTEP

For relieving any illness or disease:

DUA IMHOTEP SAKHMET THOTH

For healing with Visions:

DUA WADJET SONEB-NEFRU HOTEP

To attract First Aid, Medicine, Bandages, Compresses, or Medication (Plants):

DUA RENENUTET TA-BIJET ISHTAR

To reduce the size of Tumors, Boils or Cysts:

DUA OSIRIS-KA MONTU SAKHMET HEH

To relieve heart or other organ diseases:

DUA KHEPERI MAAT AB-NEFRU IB-NEFRU

To treat heat stroke, dehydration, fainting, low blood sugar levels, and to prevent drowning:

DUA SHU HAPY AMAM DI HOTEPU NEFRU

To avoid thoughts leading to hallucination or false memories:

DUA THOTH SESHET MAATI DI ANKH HOTEP

To heal an injury with heat energy:

DUA SET HATHOR SAKHMET DI ANKH

To punish evil fingers touching one's body:

DUA APOPHIS ISIS SAA DI ANKH HOTEPU

To punish Evil Spirits who attack one's body:

DUA KAU NEFRU AKHU DI ANKH HOTEPU

To punish Evil People who attack one's body:

DUA KHAT NEFRU AKHU DI ANKH HOTEPU

To treat Water Intoxication:

DUA HAPY DI NATRON ANKH HOTEPU

For protection during Surgery:

DUA BES AKHU KAU DI ANKH HOTEPU

To stop all illnesses or plagues:

HAIL THOTH IMHOTEP FOREVER!

To stop infections:

HAIL SESHET IMHOTEP, GIVEN OFFERINGS!

To heal injuries or cuts or open wounds:

HAIL SET, WHO GUARDS THE SKIN!

To heal internal problems, pain, or discomfort:

HAIL THOTH DUAMUTEF, FOREVER!

To stop Depressing Thoughts:

HAIL RA IN THE WINTER! HAIL BES IN THE SUMMER!

To inspire Creativity:

HAIL PTAH KHNUM FOREVER!

To request enlightenment and knowledge:

HAIL PTAH, HUSBAND OF SAKHMET, FOREVER!

To relieve Cancer symptoms:

HAIL SAKHMET AND RA FOREVER!

To relieve irritation and Diarrhea:

HAIL QEBEHSENWF AND SELQET FOREVER!

To relieve bodily pains or symptoms:

HAIL HORUS AND HATHOR FOREVER!

To stop the symptoms of Colds or Influenza:

HAIL HORUS-THE-ELDER, GUARDIAN OF PEACE!

To stop symptoms of Gall or Kidney Stones:

HAIL DUAMUTEF AND ASET (ISIS) FOREVER!

To cure or treat dry skin:

HAIL HAPY SHU TEFNUT & SESHET FOREVER!

To prevent suicidal thoughts:

HAIL BES FOREVER!

To prevent a drug overdose:

HAIL SESHET THOTH IMHOTEP GIVEN LIFE!

To prevent dangerous behavior:

HAIL SET BES HAROERIS NEPHTHYS FOREVER!

To prevent sexually transmitted diseases:

HAIL MIN HATHOR HORUS BES FOREVER!

To prevent reckless behavior:

HAIL KHNUM NEPHTHYS PTAH FOREVER!

To prevent road-rage, anger, hostility or aggression:

HAIL BES NEITH NEPHTHYS FOREVER!

Chapter 7: Love & Peace Spells

For a Peace Treaty, Truce, or Ceasefire:

DUA ASAR PAX HOTEP DI ANKH HOTEPU SHEN

For violence and hatred to end:

DUA ASAR-ISIS NEITH DI HOTEP

For music, joy, happiness:

DUA HII SESHEN HATHOR DI ANKH NEFRU

For World Peace (lasts about 24 hours):

DUA GEB HOTEP DI ANKH HOTEP HOTEPU

For people to feel Love:

DUA HATHOR VENUS APHRODITE DI ANKH

To Attract a young Maiden or Virgin:

DUA HATHOR NEFRU AA

To end all Battles and Wars:

DUA MONTU HOTEP DUA AMON HOTEP

For Mercy and Justice:

DUA MAAT MAATI HORUR HOTEP DI ANKH

For Compassion & Mercy:

DUA ALLAH-MICHAEL HOTEP DI ANKH

To preserve Civilization:

DUA ASAR DI MAAXORU HOTEP ANKH

To end plotting by Rogue States:

DUA HORUR AMONRA MAATI XA TAU

To stop Nuclear Weapons proliferation:

DUA RA HOTEP HERP TAU ANKHU

To stop the building up of foreign Armies:

DUA HORUR XA HEH NI AHAUTI TAU

To stop Hate Crimes or anger against States or their Law Enforcement:

DUA ASARIS NEFRU WENNEFER NI SET XA ANKHU

To stop all racial hatred from the Living:

DUA ANKHU NI SENA HAR XA

To thwart technology hacking or revealing of personal data:

DUA THOTH SOBEK SESHAT IMHOTEP IHY HOTEP NI KHEBENT SET XA TEP

To Prevent War(s):

DUA OSIRIS-S7 DI ANKH HOTEPU

Chapter 8: Good Actions

Give a Boat to the Shipwrecked

Lend assistance to a stranded Motorist

Clean up spilt liquids on any given floor

Clear away road-kill, debris, etc. from highways and city streets

Help the Elderly with daily maintenance

Help your procrastinating sibling with their Taxes

Tutor children in school classes (Mathematics, Computers, Literacy, History, Science, Sports, Religion, Etc.)

Stop an Arsonist, Extinguish Fires or Wildfires

Arrest a wrong-doer / Criminal / Vandal / Thief / Crook / etc.

Donate to legal Charities (Alms); give help to those who need it

Leash [or protect from] violent animals (pets)

Be courteous to others (polite, thankful, hospitable, etc.)

Ask before action

Don't stand in or block someone's way or passage

Clean up after yourself

Cook a meal for your Family

Help someone with a sickness or illness or injury

Recycle

Protect your resources: (trees, water, Energy, money)

Prevent Dehydration or Heatstroke in hot or dry weather

Cure Cancer and other malignant diseases

Protect the Environment

Control Population

Protect Ancient Monuments and Antiquities, Artifacts, etc.

Prevent the effects of Terrorism or its sanctuary

Give offerings in the Temples (to Neteru)

Be original and don't commit Plagiarism

Don't go with the flow or follow the crowd

Express yourself while mindful of others

Don't spy on your neighbors

Don't eavesdrop (unless it's about you)

Don't steal another's identity, covet their possessions, or impersonate them on the phone

Don't threaten with or commit violence or hostility in public

Don't steal, kill, or rape (i.e. commit crimes against people)

Don't abuse animals, plants, insects, etc. (Life)

Don't drink, send texting or email while driving a vehicle

Be aware of yourself while under the effects of drugs (**Don't Smoke**)

Thank your friends and associates during an Awards Presentation

Give credit where it is due

Copyright or Patent your work

Consider others' reactions to your actions

Don't over-tax the poor or middle class

Don't kill over religion or bad humor or human nature

Use Games to settle differences

Don't use Magic against Magicians

Don't use Magic (sorcery, witchcraft, etc.) against Pharaoh

Use Healing Magic to help someone

Be careful in using Telepathy on a population

Volunteer

Pray for happiness and good health / Longevity

Think positively

Be Nice to others

Don't be Crooked or value wealth over quality of work

Save a Life

Save Lives

Land a crippled airplane (vehicle) safely

Don't do anything while intoxicated (i.e. Drunk, on Drugs)

Don't create problems for others

Support Civilization

Prioritize

Be Specific

Honor your Ancestors and those worthy of adoration

Adopt

Support the Arts & Sciences

End Hunger/Obesity by balancing food resources in society

End Droughts by Water Conservation & Less Waste

Put people *before* politics

Don't damage Statues (or idols); respect other religions

Protect Cats from wild Dogs or other Cats

Protect Cats from overpopulation; donate to Animal Shelters

Care for Laboratory animals like Pets

Give Life to the Lifeless

Don't think violent thoughts

Be Efficient

Become self-sufficient (sustainable)

Be careful of New Ideas (*don't make new crimes*)

Create Museums for Artifacts

Preserve Ideas from the Past

Be friendly to "space aliens" or Extra-terrestrials

Plant a Tree (*just not endangered ones that can interfere with plumbing and cannot be removed due to State Laws*)

Be a good driver and not reckless or dangerous on the road

Be nice to your God(s)

Be a symbol of Excellence, Justice, Honesty and Integrity

Lower Radios when in public or reduce volume

Prevent Over-legislation by being Virtuous

Appreciate Wisdom of Life

Know that by avoiding all the negatives on this list you will be rich in Heaven

Know there is no reward for immorality except hot Lava in the Abyss

Know that you must have a reasonable excuse for prayers or Magic to work to one's benefit

Plan equal compensation for equal labor

Avoid Discriminating of any kind

Avoid gossip if it is not helping

Avoid Rumor mongers

Avoid Office Politics

Avoid dangerous obstacles in one's Path to Life

Avoid Pollution

Help wherever it is needed

Allow Quality over Quantity

Place Family ahead of profit or wealth

Don't surrender to Fear Politics or Terror

Don't pay ransoms to Terrorists or Rogue States

Don't duplicate crimes from television or social media

Instead of destroying excess Food or Farm products, give them to Food Banks and Charities

Avoid over-gambling or games that involve money; avoid addiction

Use Magic Sparingly (not all the time)

Build an Army for Defense, as with protection from Natural Disasters

Don't intimidate other Countries with your Military

Have a Balanced Budget in your personal life and Nation

Don't cut Core programs from your Budget because you need funding for luxury programs; needs come *before* wants

Don't have sex with relatives or your wife's sister

Don't be numb to social issues; find a solution when possible

Don't insult people based on their intellectual output or lacking thereof

Hear ideas from your superior and inferior alike

Learn Etiquette or Social Customs when traveling to a foreign culture

Always pack a First Aid Kit when traveling, even with short distances

Don't wait for bad weather to encourage you to act; be prepared in advance

Make backups of your data on separate media

Replenish bottled water to prevent bacteria from growing there

Acquire a notebook to record successes or effects of Magic

Don't light incense while on a Boat or in any area where flames can spread

Give water as an offering to the Deity in place of incense

Throw bird seeds at a wedding (not rice)

Don't torture animals or insects or birds (Life)

Enjoy some aspect of Life instead of avoiding everything in your path

Try something new

Don't allow your self-esteem from preventing possible greatness

Fear is a necessary part of living; do not indulge in it more than you can take it

It is acceptable to cry because tears release harmful chemicals from the body via the eyes

Regulate bodily fluids however this is managed

Maintain a healthy diet with moderation

Be careful of impulse-based actions

If the World must be conquered, make each former Nation into a State and give each their proper customs and ability to make Laws and Order

Unite the World in Peace so as to colonize a future World

Chapter 9: Good Divine Spirits to invoke:

Ra – the Egyptian solar God or Creator. He was worshiped at Heliopolis, and pyramids represented his body as rays coming from the sky. His secret name (M7) was once obtained by the goddess Isis, the source of his power.

Amun – the God of Air or Wind, Fertility, Conquest, and Prosperity; he was worshiped at Thebes (Waset) and Karnak.

Aton – the Solar God as the Sun itself, worshiped at Akhetaton (Tell Al-Amarna) by the Heretic Pharaoh, Akhenaton (Amonhotep 4) of late 18th Dynasty.

Ptah – Memphis Creator God, who opens the horizon's "mouth" to allow Ra to enter the sky; also venerated in the *Opening of the Mouth* ritual. Patron of Arts & Crafts, & Genetics, his name forms part of "Egypt" (in Greek, "House of the Ka of Ptah").

Sakhmet – Goddess of the hostile energy of the Sun, as in wildfires and nuclear energy. When angry she causes Natural Disasters; when happy she is invoked to cure diseases.

Nefertum – son of Ptah & Sakhmet, god of lotus flowers, music, and compassion.

Nu – God of the Primordial Abyss (Oceans), he has no temples or shrines. Nu is married to Nut, as portrayed in a *game of charades.*

Nut – Goddess of Cosmic forces (Outer Space), her body contains stars, planets, meteors, etc. She is worshiped as a protection goddess and mother goddess (Mother Nature). Sister of Geb (Seb) the Earth god.

Shu – God of Dry Heat, Hot Winds, Desert storms or sand storms. Brother of Tefnut, the goddess of rain.

Tefnut – Goddess of Moisture, rains, floods, dew, humidity, fog, storms, etc. She is the sister of Shu.

Geb (Seb) – the Earth God, he is the brother of Nut; Geb controls Earthly movements (Earthquakes, mudslides, etc.). Geb is also a name of an ancient rain god.

Osiris – Ancient Moon and Fertility god, founder of technology & civilization, son of Geb and Nut, husband of Isis, brother of Set and Nephthys, and father of Anubis and Horus. Osiris is the God of the Afterlife, Lord of Life, and Judge / Ruler of the Dead.

Anubis – Jackal god, embalmer of Osiris, Lawyer in the Court of Osiris, the Divine Physician, he is a son of Osiris.

Nephthys – Goddess of Protection (of Pharaohs) with fiery breath, sister of Osiris, mother of Anubis, wife of Set, sister of Isis, and daughter of Geb/Nut. Her crown has a building shaped like a headrest.

Isis – (**Mary**) Goddess of Magic, Protection, Fertility or Love (as Hathor), and venerated for powers of resurrection (of Osiris). She is the wife of Osiris and mother of **Horus** (**Christ**). Her crown has an "L" shaped throne on it.

Hor/us – Ancient sky god with many phases or forms of existence (many god forms of Horus), as his eyes are the Sun and Moon (Horur); he leads the righteous to Heaven after Judgement before Osiris (as **St. Michael the Archangel**), and he vanquished Set, the murderer of Osiris.

Set – Ancient god of storms and chaos, evil in general, and war. He was venerated in the 19th Dynasty as a god of war against the Hittites. He became King of Egypt after murdering Osiris and usurping his throne. He fought against Horus, eventually lost, and guarded Ra's boat in the Netherworld against the Dragon-worm Apophis as his Eternal Punishment. His color is red and his sacred animal is unknown (Tapir or Aardvark).

Ma'at – Goddess of truth, honesty, laws and order, justice, and balance; deity of creation and Cosmic Balance and Order; and a Mother Goddess. Ma'at was the wife of Thoth, daughter of Ra, and her symbol is the Ostrich feather. She is the counter balance to the heart/soul on the Scales in the Court of Osiris.

Ammot – creature that devours the failing heart at the Judgement of the Dead, Ammot is part lion, hippopotamus and with a crocodile mouth (*symbolic of heart attacks, which are attributed to poor diets in Ancient Egypt*). She sleeps near the Lake of Fire in Duat or near the Scales of Ma'at in the Court of Lord Osiris.

Maati – Twin sister of Ma'at, and related to the Judgement process.

Seshet – Goddess of literature, writing, and a historical recorder of Chronology. She assists or is married to Thoth. She assists buildings by Cosmic alignment, as in Temples. She has a crescent and star crown with 2 plumes.

Shai – Goddess of Fate and Destiny. She assists each living person from birth to the Court of Osiris, as a guide.

Selqet – Scorpion Goddess, who cures insect bites or poison; a deity of Marriage. She protects the organs in the Canopic Chest.

Sokar - God of vegetation, the Necropolis of Memphis, and of the Netherworld as a God of Death. He has a head of a (black) Hawk; associated with Osiris.

Sobek - A Crocodile God, associated with the 13th Dynasty of Kings. He is a protective deity who protects against crocodiles.

Serapis - Greek version of the Apis Bull of Memphis, and in the Serapeum in Saqqara; he was venerated by the Ptolemies in Alexandria, Egypt.

Neith - Goddess of femininity, a skilled weaver, patron deity of domestic life, and goddess of hunting, and of war. One of the 4 Canopic Goddesses protecting the organs (Isis, Nephthys, Neith & Selqet), Neith is identified with the Greek Athena, and possible mother of Ra.

Nehmauit - is a wife of Thoth ("She who uproots evil").

Nekhbet - Goddess of Protection, shown as a serpent or vulture, she is the guardian of Upper Egypt.

Uraeus - A fire-spewing (Pyrokinetic) cobra on the Crown of Ra, who destroys his enemies. He is a symbol of royalty and power.

Upuaut – Jackal God or "Opener of the Way" who protects the solar boat from enemies when traveling through Duat / The Netherworld.

Sati – first wife of Khnum, protected the upper Nile and Cataracts; she wears the white crown with 2 horns and holding archery equipment.

Khnum – ram-headed god of Upper Egypt, Creator of the bodies of humanity and the Gods on his potter's wheel; he is a god of fertility, Creation, and abundance.

Khepera – Scarab God who was the child Ra in the morning. He pushes the solar boat across the sky (*gravity holding the Sun in place*). He is a god of Creation, rebirth and Eternal Life.

Khonsu – Moon God of Thebes, son of Amun & Mut, has healing powers.

Kebehut – Daughter of Anubis, goddess of freshness.

The 7 Hathors – Clairvoyant women who protected newborns and could foresee their future.

Hathor – Wife of Hor(us), goddess of love and sexual beauty. She was represented as a cow or with cow ears. She is a solar deity with her crown having a Sun between 2 horns. She is the passive form of the Sun; the aggressive form being Sakhmet. Goddess of Joy, Music, Dancing (also attributed to Bast), and a Mother Goddess; Hathor is sometimes shown with red or blond hair, and patron of the Sycamore Tree. She was venerated at Dendera, Ombos and Edfu (See: *Temple of Hatshepsut*).

Haroeris – (Horur), Horus the Elder or Horus the Greater, this is a name of Hor(us).

Harpocrates – Horus the Child, the "god of silence."

Bast (Lady Bast) or Bastet – Cat Goddess, a fertility Goddess and protector of the home; she was venerated in Bubastis in the Delta.

Atum – the Evening form of Ra the Sun God. Atum is also a god of Creation (see *Ptah*).

M7 – abbreviated for Archangel Michael

S7 – abbreviated for a title of Osiris-Ptah

QRST – Egyptian for Christ, or "Burial."

About the Author:

Horus Michael follows the training of Ancient Egyptian Priests in his varied works on the Occult. He also studies Egyptian Archaeology. He currently lives in California, USA.

www.amazon.com/author/horusmichael

Notes: 1:

According to the King James Version of the Holy Bible, New Testament, the **main character "Jesus of Nazareth"** was born in Bethlehem under a Star while in a Manger (horse trough) on December 25. He lived for a while in Egypt until safe from an edict from a Roman Governor seeking his life. Then he moved to Nazareth and later Jerusalem. He preached and healed people later in life, following in the path of John the Baptist. Then he was captured by the Romans, tortured and crucified, died and resurrected. He lingered on Earth 40 days after the resurrection before ascending to Heaven. This data was written centuries *after* these events took place. Jesus was said to have fulfilled prophecies about the Israelite Messiah. But no records exist *outside of* the Bible to verify any of this information. All we have are religious sources and artifacts created afterwards. We must accept this on faith. So what is the real information? Let's find out.

The Ancient Egyptian Calendar was 360 days comprised of 10 day work weeks without a weekend or break. The Israelite Prophet Moses created the Weekend by saying God created for 6 days and rested on the 7th.

At the end of 360 days are added 5 *Epagomenal Days* to even the year to 365 days. These are the **birthdays** of Osiris, Horus, Set, Isis, and Nephthys. There are **3 Seasons: Flooding, Harvest and Planting Seasons**. Flooding is mid July to November; Harvest is mid November until March; Planting is mid March to July. Flood Season begins with New Year's Day, 1 week after the Summer Solstice. Planting is around the Spring Equinox (Easter). Harvest is during Winter Solstice. These Seasons are via the Egyptian God, Lord Osiris, who invented Agriculture and Civilization.

Lord Osiris was the (legendary) first King of Egypt's pre-dynastic era, in Upper Egypt. He created Civilization in Egypt then conquered the rest of the World and civilized them. He is remembered by other names in many cultures. He returned to Egypt afterwards and attended a party in his honor, wherein his envious younger brother Set killed Osiris in a Magic trick involving a chest, and then usurped the throne. Osiris floated downstream in the chest to Byblos, where the box was entangled in a Cedar tree. His wife Isis found him there, as the tree was cut down into a pillar for a king in the region. The tree was opened and revealed his body. The Cedar wood scent is his dying flesh.

Isis fanned wind into Osiris with her angelic wings. This resurrected Osiris. Then he mated with Isis and sister Nephthys before returning to Egypt to challenge Set's rule.

Set was the usurper of the throne and ruled Egypt with an iron fist. He outlawed vegetarian diets from Osiris, inspired meat eating (Human flesh and pork), and controlled earthquakes and storms with his will. Set was also a god of war and chaos/evil. His sacred color is Red (Planet Mars).

Osiris had 2 sons *after* resurrection – Horus and Anubis. When Osiris returned to Egypt to challenge Set, he was again murdered and this time he was dismembered to make it difficult to resurrect. His body parts were scattered along the Nile River, so Isis had to hunt for these parts while Horus battled Set for dominion. Horus and Isis fled into the Delta initially where he ruled until he was strong enough to challenge the usurper. When Isis found a part, she erected a shrine or temple to mark its place. His head was found in Abydos, and his body was later interred in a mountain near the Valley of the Kings.

The battles of Horus and Set were well recorded. This is similar to St. Michael vs. Satan, or Hercules vs. the Dragon (constellation).

Horus battled Set and lost his eyes, later repaired by Thoth; one was called the Wadjet Eye or *"Eye of Sacrifice"* and was used as an offering to Osiris by Horus in the *Opening of the Mouth* ceremony.

Later the final battle was in the **Court room of Lord Osiris**, as King of Heaven, whereby each participant presented their case on who was worthy to be king. Set lost and was beheaded as a result. His soul now protects the Boat of Ra when it visits the Netherworld from the Worm of Apophis. Osiris is the Judge of the actions of the Living. The actions determine worthiness to be an Angel or live in Heaven after physical death. **Osiris is the King of Kings**, the Ruler of Rulers, and Lord of Lords; the Divine ruler of the Living, and supreme sovereign of the Universe. He was worshiped up until the Christian era of the Roman Empire that replaced his worship with Christianity. Osiris said, "Whosoever believes in me will endure forever." His sacred food is bread and wine, or bread and beer for commoners. He was buried in a tomb, so he became the **first Christ**, or in Egyptian the word is **QRST**, meaning "Burial." Christ means "anointed" as in Egyptian Mummification process that the body is anointed with perfumed oils to purify it.

The Christian Calendar moved the birthday of Jesus from **June 25** (5 days after Summer Solstice) to 5 days after the Winter Solstice (Dec. 20) and then one week before New Years. This was to **separate the idea** from being a solar religion. His birthday is *still* a birthday *after* the Solstice.

The Christians replaced all ideology about solar and lunar Egyptian ideas with Jesus. Christianity was seen as *Romanized* or updated Osiris worship. For Jesus is a Judge of the Living, the King of Kings, the Prince of Peace, and other attributes of Osiris worship. He was even buried in a tomb and resurrected. The *Eye of Sacrifice* was the **Body of Christ**, sacrificed for the sins of the living; represented in ritual the bread and wine offerings for Osiris (Eucharist, Communion).

Jesus was a Carpenter in the Bible. But he was too poor as a Carpenter to afford expensive things like red wine or spikenard perfume, especially with a vow of poverty. People in the Ancient World used perfume and water until the invention of soap for purification. Jesus would "wash people's feet" or baptize them to purify their souls. He also exorcised "unclean spirits" (Diseases).

In Egyptian religion, the Lector Priest (**Kheri-Heb**) used a Carpenter's tool (Adze) in the performance of the *Opening of the Mouth* ceremony. The Lector Priest also could resurrect the dead, and make storms or earthquakes using Egyptian Magic/Science. A Priest of Sakhmet, the Goddess of Natural Disasters and healing, could heal people with supernatural power. A priest would start with a lower position such as a Purification Priest, by immersing people in water (Baptism initiation rites).

The period for Mummification was 40 days. This is followed by a Night Boat ritual whereby the soul ascended to Heaven/the stars.

In Christian doctrine, there were Wise Men who attended Christ's birth, and gave 3 offerings of gold, frankincense and myrrh. So most people believe this was "3 Wise Men" or "3 Kings." **If this is correct**, the 3 Kings represented the 3 Pyramids at Giza, as built by 3 Kings = Khufu (Cheops in Greek), Khafre (Chephren) and Menkaura (Mycerinus). The 3 Kings "followed" the star to the Manger in Bethlehem. The Manger or Horse Trough is the trapezoid shaped Mastaba of Shepseskaf in Saqqara, Egypt.

The Mastaba is a tomb shaped like a trapezoid or Manger. This was the last King of the 4th Dynasty (the Giza Pyramids were also 4th Dynasty). Inside the tomb were grave goods – hence, "gold, frankincense and myrrh." **Jesus was named after Djedkara-Isesi,** or was the King named that, and his life was celebrated or made into this legend? Djed-Ka-Ra Isesi has a pyramid temple nearby. The Roman spelling of Jesus is "IESUS." The Egyptian word is "ISESI" or "IZEZI." Egyptologists place an "e" in between consonants in transcribing names, so ISESI would be I-E-S-E-S-I, or IESIS or IESUS. Vowels are not written. (or *Iesesi Lives*).

The King named Djed-Ka-Ra Isesi was found in the 1940s; he was about 50 to 60 years of age and ruled about 44 years. His parents are unknown but he had children. He was from the 5th Dynasty. He led expeditions to Nubia for **gold** and in Punt for **myrrh** incense, also in Sinai for turquoise and copper. He led raids in Canaan (modern Israel). He also had reforms in the government and was celebrated in later generations. His vizier was the famous sage Ptah-hotep. If this was the inspiration for Jesus of Nazareth, Ptah-hotep's Maxims would represent **Wisdom.** Other Pharaohs are also possible, such as *King Tutankhamon.*

The 3 Kings followed to the King Shepseskaf of the 4th Dynasty, that is, they ruled *before* he did. **Bethlehem** means in Hebrew and Aramaic "**House of Bread**:"

The House of Bread is the symbol for Invocation Offerings or an Offerings Chamber inside a tomb (Mastaba). The Star of his birth would be a Pyramid as seen from a distance with a golden capstone, or a painted star on the ceiling of the tomb. The 3 stars of Orion represent the Giza Pyramids as seen in the sky. If you can trace the distance in the sky for Orion, the "star" of Bethlehem would point to the location of the Mastaba as seen on the ground. People used star maps for directions in ancient times.

Now Jesus' mother Mary was a "Virgin" (*Youthful*) and was "with child *before* meeting Joseph." The Virgo Constellation in the night sky would be the location of the Star of his birth. Joseph was **not** his *biological father*, so Jesus is not related to King David. The Virgin may mean something else entirely.

Vestal Virgins in Rome were priestesses of Vesta. They were unmarried women who were chaste and pure. If they became pregnant it was considered a major sin. Romans would pursue a rogue Vestal if this happened. So Mary married Joseph in Egypt to escape this situation or persecution, not Herod's alleged edict about the Christ. The father was unknown, and conspicuous. So naturally it was seen as "from god." If a spirit or deity impregnated Mary with *Astral Sperm*, then this explains why Jesus was supernatural. It also represents that the "father of Jesus" is Jesus when he said "My Father and I are one" (**John 10:30**); so he made her pregnant upon entering her and stayed there until birth. This happens during sleep.

Joseph's position in Egypt would be as a priest – "**God's Father" title**. The offerings of gold, frankincense, and myrrh are a **wedding dowry**. Jesus is either named after Pharaoh **Isesi** or *Djoser* (*The Holy One* – Mark 1:24). Joseph can be written "Shep-ses-kaf" after the Mastaba's owner (Jo-Shep...). Mary would be "Merit" in Egyptian, the word for Love (MRY).

The accuracy of the Old Testament is questionable. In Genesis 42 the Israelites "buy grain in Egypt with Silver Money." (Genesis 45:22). In Genesis 45:19 wagons are loaded with goods in Egypt. Now **silver money was not invented until** at least 680 BCE, and wagons (4 wheeled types) did not exist in Egypt, only 2 wheeled chariots. Also the Bible never mentions the Conquest of Israel by Pharaoh Merenptah, the son of Pharaoh Ramses the Great – thought by some to be the *Exodus Pharaoh* on account of his name. If the Bible was written in Ancient times, this major event would be in it. Rather it could be written in later Roman Empire era, when wagons and silver money existed. Greek silver coin money was invented around 500 BCE and imported to Egypt by Alexander the Great in 332 BCE. Ramses the Great lived in about 1200 BCE. Tutankhamon lived in 1330 BCE. Silver in Egypt was more valuable than gold, not likely to be used as currency. You would be very wealthy if you had "300 pieces of silver money" in Ancient Egypt. The roadways in Egypt consisted of water canals linked to the Nile as its main highway. Chariots were rare due to a lack of horses. 4 wheeled vehicles existed in Sumer or Babylon, led by donkeys or mules.

Notes: 2:

Jesus said unto him, if you can believe, all things are possible to him that believes.

Mark 9:23

The act of divine utterance is found in the Egyptian Creator Ptah, who creates by speaking, or Thoth who creates by writing, or Horus who is the voice of Ptah. **Power** is conferred after successful **building up of authority in a person.** You must **believe** you are higher than a commoner, for the energy to be handled wisely. The spirits who occupy Space do not know you; you must convince them that you are their ally and friend. These spirits control all aspects of Nature, Humanity, the Afterlife, and living creatures. They control the wind, rain, snow, earth movements, fire, solar flame, and human actions in the future.

Jesus acquired authority first, and then his powers became real. Once this was done, he could cast out "unclean spirits" to cure diseases and heal people. If angered, he killed a fig plant or was upset that a woman touched his robe, and she was cured, but *not by him* or his power. Sometimes the **power to believe** is the answer, for this enables the Soul or Mind or Ka Spirit to act in the World. By not believing, nothing will happen. **Atheists do not believe, so they cause nothing.** This ability is called Magic in Egypt, Sorcery in the East, Miracles of God in the Bible, or Psychic Powers in the West.

To master his abilities took time, from inception in Egypt, to the secret years after age 12 until we first hear him heal people as an adult. He healed thousands of people, and gathered together many followers, and even resurrected himself after his execution. The spirits who he engendered in peace and friendship caused these events.

His authority was the Christ (QRST), the Son of God, the Prince of Peace, the King of Kings, etc. These **attributes** were taken from Egyptian Gods, while he lived in Egypt as a child or youth. The Bible does not say what he did while in Egypt. But by **age 12** he was highly educated when he impressed the people in the Temple with his knowledge. It was in Egypt where he learned to develop his powers, just as Moses did.

Belief and Prayer are mental functions. The mind can perform powerful actions when fully explored by the courageous. **Prayer causes Telepathy** by thinking in great amounts until your thoughts escapes the brain and radiate outwards to other people. Thinking to someone or about someone is **Christian Prayer**. Jesus taught you Egyptian Magic and Psychic Power under the guise of religion. Positive Prayers heal; negative prayers destroy. Authority with energy focuses in prayer and can cause future events.

The Egyptians used statues or idols to focus their energy. Later civilizations used books or stories about magical people.

According to the King James Version of the Holy Bible, New Testament, the **main character "Jesus of Nazareth"** was born in Bethlehem under a Star while in a Manger (horse trough) on December 25. He lived for a while in Egypt until safe from an edict from a Roman Governor seeking his life. Then he moved to Nazareth and later Jerusalem. He preached and healed people later in life, following in the path of John the Baptist. Then he was captured by the Romans, tortured and crucified, died and resurrected. He lingered on Earth 40 days after the resurrection before ascending to Heaven. This data was written centuries *after* these events took place. Jesus was said to have fulfilled prophecies about the Israelite Messiah. But no records exist *outside of* the Bible to verify any of this information. All we have are religious sources and artifacts created afterwards. We must accept this on faith. So what is the real information? Let's find out.

The Ancient Egyptian Calendar was 360 days comprised of 10 day work weeks without a weekend or break. The Israelite Prophet Moses created the Weekend by saying God created for 6 days and rested on the 7th.

At the end of 360 days are added **5 *Epagomenal Days*** to even the year to 365

days. These are the **birthdays** of Osiris,
Horus, Set, Isis, and Nephthys. There are **3
Seasons: Flooding, Harvest and Planting
Seasons**. Flooding is mid July to November;
Harvest is mid November until March; Planting
is mid March to July. Flood Season begins
with New Year's Day, after the Summer
Solstice. Planting is around the Spring
Equinox (Easter). Harvest is during Winter
Solstice. These Seasons are via the Egyptian
God, Lord Osiris, who invented Agriculture
and Civilization. Flooding is the Lamentation
of Osiris, Planting is the resurrection of Osiris,
and Harvest is the death of Osiris.

Lord Osiris was the (legendary) **first
King of Egypt's** pre-dynastic era, in Upper
Egypt. He created Civilization in Egypt then
conquered the rest of the World **and civilized
them**. He is remembered **by other names** in
many cultures. He returned to Egypt
afterwards and attended a party in his honor,
wherein his envious younger brother Set killed
Osiris in a Magic trick involving a chest, and
then usurped the throne. Osiris floated
downstream in the chest to Byblos, where the
box was entangled in a Cedar tree. His wife
Isis found him there, as the tree was cut down
into a pillar for a king in the region. The tree
was opened and revealed his body. The Cedar
wood scent is his dying flesh.

Isis fanned wind into Osiris with her **angelic wings.** This resurrected Osiris. Then he mated with Isis and sister Nephthys before returning to Egypt to challenge Set's rule.

Set was the usurper of the throne and ruled Egypt with an iron fist. He outlawed vegetarian diets from Osiris, inspired meat eating (Human flesh and pork), and controlled earthquakes and storms with his will. Set was also a god of war and chaos/evil. His sacred color is Red (Planet Mars).

Osiris had 2 sons *after* resurrection – Horus and Anubis. When Osiris returned to Egypt to challenge Set, he was again murdered and this time he was dismembered to make it difficult to resurrect. His body parts were scattered along the Nile River, so Isis had to hunt for these parts while Horus battled Set for dominion. Horus and Isis fled into the Delta initially where he ruled until he was strong enough to challenge the usurper. When Isis found a part, she erected a shrine or temple to mark its place. His head was found in Abydos, and his body was later interred in a mountain near the Valley of the Kings.

The battles of Horus and Set were well recorded. This is similar to St. Michael vs. Satan, or Hercules vs. the Dragon (Constellation).

Horus battled Set and lost his eyes, later repaired by Thoth; one was called the Wadjet Eye or *"Eye of Sacrifice"* and was used as an offering to Osiris by Horus in the *Opening of the Mouth* ceremony.

Later the final battle was in the **Court room of Lord Osiris**, as King of Heaven, whereby each participant presented their case on who was worthy to be king. Set lost and was beheaded as a result. His soul now protects the Boat of Ra when it visits the Netherworld from the Worm of Apophis. Osiris is the Judge of the actions of the Living. The actions determine worthiness to be an **Angel** or live in Heaven after physical death. **Osiris is the King of Kings**, the Ruler of Rulers, and Lord of Lords; he is the Divine ruler of the Living, and Supreme Sovereign of the Universe. He was worshiped up until the Christian era of the Roman Empire that replaced his worship with Christianity. Osiris said, "Whosoever believes in me will endure forever." His sacred food is bread and wine, or bread and beer for commoners. He was buried in a tomb, so he became the **first Christ**, or in Egyptian the word is **QRST (KRST)**, meaning "Burial." Christ means "anointed" as in Egyptian Mummification process that the body is anointed with perfumed oils to purify it. Christ was also buried in a tomb.

The Christian Calendar moved the birthday of Jesus from **June 25** (5 days after Summer Solstice) to 5 days after the Winter Solstice (Dec. 20) and then one week before New Years. This was to **separate the idea** from being a solar religion. His birthday is *still* a birthday *after* the Solstice.

The Christians replaced all ideology about solar and lunar Egyptian ideas with Jesus. **Christianity** was seen as *Romanized* or **updated Osiris worship**. For Jesus is a Judge of the Living, the King of Kings, the Prince of Peace, and other attributes of Osiris worship.

He was even buried in a tomb and resurrected. The *Eye of Sacrifice* was the **Body of Christ**, sacrificed for the sins of the living; represented in ritual the bread and wine ('Awa) offerings for Osiris (Eucharist, Communion).

Jesus was a **Carpenter** in the Bible. But he was too poor as a Carpenter to afford expensive things like red wine or spikenard perfume, especially with a vow of poverty. People in the Ancient World used perfume and water until the invention of soap for purification. Jesus would "wash people's feet" or baptize them to purify their souls. He also exorcised "unclean spirits" (Diseases). So how did he afford to buy these items, unless he was actually a Priest in Egypt?

In Egyptian religion, the Lector Priest (**Kheri-Heb**) used a **Carpenter's** tool (**Adze**) in the performance of the *Opening of the Mouth* ceremony. The Lector Priest also could resurrect the dead, and make storms or earthquakes using Egyptian Magic/Science. A Priest of Sakhmet, the Goddess of Natural Disasters and healing, could heal people with supernatural power. A priest would start with a lower position such as a Purification Priest, by immersing people in water (*Baptism initiation rites*).

The period for Mummification was 40 days. This is followed by a Night Boat ritual whereby the soul ascended to Heaven/the stars.

In Christian doctrine, there were Wise Men who attended Christ's birth, and gave 3 offerings of gold, frankincense and myrrh. So most people believe this was **"3 Wise Men" or "3 Kings." If this is correct**, the 3 Kings represented the 3 Pyramids at Giza, as built by 3 Kings = Khufu (Cheops in Greek), Khafre (Chephren) and Menkaura (Mycerinus). The 3 Kings "followed" the star to the Manger in Bethlehem. The **Manger** or Horse Trough **is the** trapezoid shaped **Mastaba of Shepseskaf in Saqqara, Egypt.**

The Mastaba is a tomb shaped like a trapezoid or Manger. This was the last King of the 4ᵗʰ Dynasty (the Giza Pyramids were also 4ᵗʰ Dynasty). Inside the tomb were grave goods – hence, "gold, frankincense and myrrh." **Jesus was named after Djedkara-Isesi,** or was the King named that, and his life was celebrated or made into this legend? Djed-Ka-Ra Isesi has a pyramid temple nearby. The Roman spelling of Jesus is "IESUS." The Egyptian word is "ISESI" or "IZEZI." Egyptologists place an "e" in between consonants in transcribing names, so ISESI would be I-E-S-E-S-I, or IESIS or IESUS. Vowels are not written.

The King named Djed-Ka-Ra Isesi was found in the 1940s; he was about 50 to 60 years of age and ruled about 44 years. His parents are unknown but he had children. He was from the 5ᵗʰ Dynasty. He led expeditions to Nubia for **gold** and in Punt for **myrrh** incense, also in Sinai for turquoise and copper. He led raids in Canaan (modern Israel). He also had reforms in the government and was celebrated in later generations. His vizier was the famous sage **Ptah-hotep**. If this was the inspiration for Jesus of Nazareth, Ptah-hotep's Maxims would represent **Wisdom**. Other Pharaohs are also possible, such as *King Tutankhamon*.

The 3 Kings followed to the King Shepseskaf of the 4th Dynasty, that is, they ruled *before* he did. **Bethlehem** means in Hebrew and Aramaic "**House of Bread**:"

The **House of Bread is** the symbol for Invocation Offerings or **an Offerings Chamber** inside a tomb (Mastaba). The Star of his birth would be a Pyramid as seen from a distance with a golden capstone, or a painted star on the ceiling of the tomb. The 3 stars of Orion represent the Giza Pyramids as seen in the sky. If you can trace the distance in the sky for Orion, the "star" of Bethlehem would point to the location of the Mastaba as seen on the ground. People used star maps for directions in ancient times.

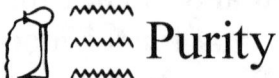 Purity

Now Jesus' mother Mary was a "Virgin" and was "with child *before* meeting Joseph." The Virgo Constellation in the night sky would be the location of the Star of his birth. Joseph was **not** his *biological father*, so Jesus is **not related to** King David. The Virgin may mean something else entirely.

Vestal Virgins in Rome were priestesses of Vesta. They were unmarried women who were chaste and pure. If they became pregnant it was considered a major sin. Romans would pursue a rogue Vestal if this happened. So Mary married Joseph in Egypt to escape this situation or persecution, not Herod's alleged edict about the Christ. The father was unknown, and conspicuous. So naturally it was seen as "from god." If a spirit or deity impregnated Mary with *Astral Sperm*, then this explains why Jesus was supernatural. It also represents that the "father of Jesus" *is Jesus* when he said "My Father and I are one" (**John 10:30**); so he made her pregnant upon entering her and stayed there until birth. This happens during sleep.

Joseph's position in Egypt would be as a priest – "**God's Father**" **title**. The offerings of gold, frankincense, and myrrh are a **wedding dowry**. Jesus is either named after Pharaoh **Isesi** or *Djoser* (*The Holy One* – Mark 1:24). Joseph can be written "Shep-ses-kaf" after the Mastaba's owner (Jo-Shep...). Mary would be "Merit" in Egyptian, the word for Love (MRY).

The accuracy of the Old Testament is questionable. In Genesis 42 the Israelites "buy grain in Egypt with Silver Money." (Genesis 45:22). In Genesis 45:19 wagons are loaded with goods in Egypt. Now **silver money was not invented until** at least 680 BCE, and wagons (4 wheeled types) did not exist in Egypt, only 2 wheeled chariots. Also the Bible never mentions the Conquest of Israel by Pharaoh Merenptah, the son of Pharaoh Ramses the Great – thought by some to be the *Exodus Pharaoh* on account of his name. If the Bible was written in Ancient times, this major event would be in it. Rather it could be written in later Roman Empire era, when wagons and silver money existed. Greek silver coin money was invented around 500 BCE and imported to Egypt by Alexander the Great in 332 BCE. Ramses the Great lived in about 1200 BCE. Tutankhamon lived in 1330 BCE. Silver in Egypt was more valuable than gold, not likely to be used as currency. You would be very wealthy if you had "300 pieces of silver money" in Ancient Egypt. The roadways in Egypt consisted of water canals linked to the Nile as its main highway. Chariots were rare due to a lack of horses. 4 wheeled vehicles existed in Sumer or Babylon, led by donkeys or mules.

Bibliography:

The Complete Temples of Ancient Egypt
© Richard H. Wilkinson, 2000 T&H, ISBN: 0-500-05100-3.

Amulets of Ancient Egypt © Carol
Andrews 1994, University of Texas Press, ISBN: 0-292-704640-X

Magic in Ancient Egypt © Geraldine
Pinch, 1994 University of Texas Press, ISBN: 0-292-76559-2

How to read Egyptian Hieroglyphs – a step-by-step guide to teach yourself © Mark
Collier, Bill Manley, 1998 University of California Press, ISBN: 0-965-69303-1

The Ancient Egyptian Book of the Dead
© R. O. Faulkner, 1997 University of Texas Press, ISBN: 0-292-7042509

The Book of Opening of the Mouth ©
E.A. Wallis Budge, volume 1. ISBN: 9780548127285

The British Museum Book of Ancient Egypt, © Stephen Quirke & Jeffrey Spencer, 1992, ISBN: 0-500-27902-0

The Complete Tutankhamun – The King, the tomb, the royal treasure © Nicholas
Reeves, 1990. ISBN: 0-500-27810-5.

Ancient Egyptian Myths & Legends © Lewis Spence, 1990. ISBN: 0-486-26525-0.

College of Egyptian Magic © Horus Michael 2016. ISBN: 9781539624622.

Templar Knighthood: Psychic Warfare 101: Combating Terror with Egyptian Magic © Iesu Nazareth (Horus Michael) 2016. ISBN: 9781534775138.

An Egyptian Priest Magicianary © Horus Michael, 2016. ISBN: 9781523606566.

Pharaohism – The official religion of Ancient Egypt, © Michael J. Costa, 2014. ISBN: 9781495284137.

Sakhmet's Effective Egyptian Magic Spells: Revised Edition © Horus Michael, 2014. ISBN: 9781505446074.

The Holy Bible – King James Version

The American Research Center in Egypt © ARCE www.arce.org

PBS (Television); The History Channel

The House of the Messiah © **Ahmed Osman 1992**; *The Church of Tutankhamon* © 2015 HM

My Life & Prophecies © Jeane Dixon 1969.

If the mummy in KV55 is Akhenaton, why is it in a Coffin or Mummy Case? Akhenaton was *against Osiris worship*, and the Coffin / Mummy was associated with Osiris only. Atonism did not favor association with the Traditional religions. So it doesn't matter the age of the mummy, just its container.

If Tutankhamon is the "bodily son of Akhenaton" **why doesn't he** strongly resemble Akhenaton from the known sculptures? If Tut was the son of Nefertiti the double-chin line would have merit, unless he obtained this trait from Queen Meritaton, the *daughter* of Nefertiti. Tut is not deformed enough to be the *Bodily Son of the Heretic Pharaoh*.

 QRST

The **sedative** Jesus drank before "giving up the ghost" / passing out while crucified, could be related to *Morphine* from **Poppy plants.** This would slow his heartbeat so as to appear dead. No one ever died on the first day of being crucified, so this is suspicious. Most died from exposure to the elements, weeks later.

Now in disproving the Bible leaves the door open to analyze other religions that *based their ideas on* the Hebrew Book, like Islam or Baha'i. In Islam, Jesus was seen as a Prophet, and would return to Earth as a Muslim (wishful thinking). If Jesus is a Prophet, what then of Osiris? Osiris had real resurrections, where Jesus faked his death on the cross, just to claim he resurrected as part of the belief system he was building.

Islam also based the Judgement of the Dead and the Resurrection in the Quran. The Judgement was taken directly from Osiris worship. Praying five times a day in Islam was said to be part of a *solar religion* as no Muslim prayed at night. Surrendering to God in prayer was taken from the act of *"kissing the floor before Pharaoh"* in Ancient Egypt and in the Persian Empire when Alexander the Great conquered them. Islamic head wraps are from *Nemes* head clothes of Ancient Egyptian Pharaohs, not just from Desert Arabs. Green, the color of Islam, is one of two colors associated with Lord Osiris (green & black). Osiris also has a beard, like most Muslims. Both had a strict moral code of life.

Notes: 4:

(St. Matthew 1:16)

"And Jacob begat Joseph, **the husband of Mary**, of whom was born JESUS, who is called Christ."

Jesus was born of Mary, **not the son of Joseph,** because it is written that Jesus was the "Son of God." So he is not related to King David biologically, but only via his **step-father** Joseph, the husband of Mary. Mary was with child *before* meeting him **(Matthew 1:18)**. We know only the supernatural element via dreams or Psychic visions.

(St. Matthew 2:1-10)

Who had a vision of the King of the Jews prior to the birth, and who told the "Wise Men" about this event?

(St. Matthew 2:15)

"...Out of **Egypt** have I called **my son**."

This indicates **the Son of God is Egyptian, not Hebrew.** Otherwise it would have said, "Out of Israel have I called my son." **In Egypt**, Pharaohs are called the **Son of** (this **God**) Ra, or descended from the gods.

(St. Matthew 2:23)

    The City of Nazareth is where Jesus lived. The Egyptian word for God is NTR or Neter; some versions are NTJR or **Netjer**. TJ is similar in use as DJ in Egyptian Hieroglyphs; both can be rendered as a "Z" – NZR or **Nezer** (from TJ or DJ to Z).

    (From Na**tz**erath); unknown origin.

http://www.dictionary.com/browse/nazareth

    If the words have unknown origins, would the original word be Egyptian *before* the cities are named in Israel?

(St. Matthew 3:16-17)

    A spirit like a dove entered Jesus after immersion in the waters:

    A human soul is white, the Ba (soul) is like a bird that comes and goes from Earth to Heaven. This is evidence that there is nothing of spiritual importance regarding Jesus' Baptism.

(St. Matthew 4:1-3)

    If you go without food for 40 days and nights, of course you will have hallucinations. This is the spiritual equivalent of *Boot Camp* in the Army.

(St. Matthew 6:7)

"**Prayer with repetitions** by the Heathens" **is a reference to Ancient Egyptian Prayers.** It is not repeating the prayers that make it heard, rather it is the short amount of time it will take to work if repeated.

(St. Matthew 6:11 – The Lord's Prayer)

"Give us this day our daily bread"

In Egypt bread was made daily. You would think there was more food readily available by the time of the Roman Empire than bread. Egypt supplied Grain to Rome after Octavian acquired Egypt.

(St. Matthew 6:24)

*"No man can serve two Masters...Ye cannot serve God and **Mammon**."*

This appears to be a **corruption of Amon**, though Amen is used at the end of Christian Prayers, and **Ammon** is a reference to the Greek use of **Amon from Siwa Oasis in Egypt**. Amon was the God of Wealth and Treasures, or "God of the Poor" because he was worshiped to supply material delights. He was also worshiped as the King of the Gods as **AmonRa**, of air/wind, conquest, and fertility.

https://en.wikipedia.org/wiki/Mammon

Was Jesus an Egyptian Pharaoh?

He was born in an Offerings Chamber ("Bethlehem, House of Bread") in a Mastaba ("Manger") tomb (QRST) with funerary offerings of Gold, Frankincense and Myrrh. Three Kings followed him (3 Kings of Giza Pyramids, 4th Dynasty Egypt) to the Star of his birth. He was named after an Egyptian Pharaoh (Isisi) whose Pyramid was nearby in Saqqara, Egypt, the location of the Mastaba tomb. He was a Son of God (Son of Ra) and King of Kings (Osiris). He was a Carpenter (Lector Priest using an adze or Carpenter's tool). He was rich enough to afford Red Wine and Spikenard Perfume (only royalty used it). He was the styled King of the Jews (originated from Egypt), and "God said, Out of Egypt have I called my son." He was crucified and resurrected, and then he lingered for 40 days until ascending to Heaven, which is **code** for being mummified and the night boat ritual whereby the soul is united with Heaven. He washed people's feet (Purification Priest ritual or hieroglyph for Purity). He was Baptized before his Ministry began (immersion into water in a Temple pool or lake, also initiation rite in Egypt). He had 12 followers (12 months of the year/ Zodiac) with him in the Center (as Ra). He was a Shepherd (Pharaoh). He healed people (Priest of Sakhmet). His birth is celebrated on a day from the Egyptian / Julian Calendar converted to the Christian Calendar.

www.ingramcontent.com/pod-product-compliance
Lightning Source LLC
Chambersburg PA
CBHW060300290526
45789CB00001B/367